Braving the Street
The Anthropology of Homelessness

PUBLIC ISSUES IN ANTHROPOLOGICAL PERSPECTIVE
General Editors: William Beeman and David Kertzer, Department of
Anthropology, Brown University

Original sketch of homeless man by Jason Glasser

Braving the Street

The Anthropology of Homelessness

Irene Glasser and *Rae Bridgman*

Berghahn Books
New York • Oxford

First published in 1999 by
Berghahn Books

Library of Congress Cataloging-in-Publication Data
Glasser, Irene.
  Braving the street : the anthropology of homelessness / by Irene Glasser
and Rae Bridgman.
          p.   cm. -- (Public isues in anthropological perspective : v. 1)
       ISBN 1-57181-096-X (hardback : alk. paper)
       ISBN 1-57181-097-8 (paperback : alk. paper)
       1. Homelessness--United States.   2. Homelessness--Canada.
  I. Bridgman, Rae.   II. Title.   III. Series.
  HV4505.G53   1999   98-47284
  362.5'0973--dc21   CIP

British Library Cataloguing in Publication Data
A catalogue record for this book is available from the British Library.

Contents

List of
Tables and Figures,
Photos and Illustrations

Acknowledgements

We would like to gratefully acknowledge our family, friends, and colleagues, who have sustained us through the creative process of writing this book.

Irene would like to thank her loving family – children, Jason, Raphael, Jonathan, and Nathaniel; husband Morty; parents, Charlotte and Gerald Biederman; and brother, Michael.

Rae would like to thank her beloved family – husband Winston; children, Jennie, Izak, Aengus, Ezra, Hanah, and Amos, and parents, Lois and David Anderson.

Irene thanks her friends, Anna, Hydie, Gayle, Joy, Edith, Jane, Patrick, and Marianna, and mentor, Dr. Pertti J. Pelto.

Gracias por todo, Rabino Alejandro.

Un merci spécial à mes amis montréalais : Louise, André, et Micheline.

Rae thanks her colleagues, Terri Aihoshi, Kathy M'Closkey, Lynne Milgram, Margaret Rodman, and Penny van Esterik for their ongoing support.

Irene is grateful for the support she received from the Connecticut State University Research Foundation, the Eastern Connecticut State University (ECSU) School of Arts and Sciences Released Time, and the Academic Relations Program of the Canadian Consulate in New York and the Canadian Embassy in Washington D.C., all of which were instrumental in the research and writing of this book. Thanks also to Jennifer Alexanian, her excellent research assistant. As always, thanks to the ECSU library staff for facilitating this research.

Rae gratefully acknowledges support from the Social Sciences and Humanities Research Council of Canada through two Strategic Grants [Women and Change].

We both thank the editors of the series, William Beeman and David Kertzer, for inviting us to write this book. We also thank publisher Marion Berghahn for her dedication to bringing interesting and timely books into print.

We will be donating a portion of any profits from this book to community development projects that fight homelessness.

Preface

With this volume we believe that anthropology's place as a major contributor to research on homelessness in North America will be firmly established. The knowledge gathered by anthropologists suggests varying strategies for easing the lives of those who are homeless, and contributes to the still greater project, preventing and eradicating homelessness. Just as anthropology has become important in confronting world problems such as AIDS and malnutrition, so too has it focused attention on the plight of those without shelter. Anthropology's methodologies, theories, and modes of analysis make it especially suited to unearthing the subtleties of problems that arise as societies adapt to the complexities of contemporary life.

Anthropologists have long worked in poverty subcultures within North America. Earlier works, such as Elliot Liebow's *Tally's Corner*, John Spradley's *You Owe Yourself a Drunk*, Carol Stack's *All Our Kin*, and the work of Oscar Lewis (*La Vida, Children of Sanchez*), laid the groundwork for the current research on homelessness. In addition to these in-depth studies, there are ethnographically rich descriptions of squatter settlements, street children, and pavement dwellers from elsewhere in the world.

As authors, we bring several different perspectives to our work. Glasser provides a view from the United States, where homelessness is regarded as an almost intractable problem. It is seen as the end result of decades of social policies that have ignored the deterioration of most of the nation's cities, and have retreated from guarantees of a minimum standard of living. Glasser's extensive experience and observations come from a number of qualitative and quantitative research studies, which she conducted on poverty-related issues, including soup kitchens, welfare, mothers in prison, and homelessness. At times she has observed people giving up the very *idea* of ever having a place of their own. She has also systematically researched the phenomenon of homelessness in world perspective, writing about its shifting conceptualizations around the globe.

Bridgman represents a point of view informed by the Canadian experience with homelessness, which appears to be less severe in terms of numbers of people affected than in the U.S. Homelessness in Canada has also only relatively recently been recognized as a problem, and there is far less published material on homelessness in Canada than in the U.S. Canada is, moreover, well-known for its universal social programs (the health-care system is perhaps the best known) which guarantee a minimum standard of living. This guarantee extends to the concept of "social housing," a term that is not in everyday parlance in the U.S. Bridgman's observations come from extended case-study research documenting the efforts of many different constituents (homeless people, service providers, government officials, municipal administrators, and others) involved in developing innovative projects to tackle chronic homelessness.

We both believe that anthropology has much to contribute to the general public's knowledge of homelessness, and that anthropologists can help to light the way for creative approaches to the problem. We seek to explore issues of homelessness from many points of view. We are presenting you, the reader, with what we believe to be the best information about homelessness garnered throughout the world. We stress the point of view of those inside the culture (the "native" or "emic" point of view, as anthropologists refer to it), and thus we view the homeless in a very heterogeneous way. We see strengths and organization at times when others see chaos. However, we also see lives cut short by the rigors of the street, and we dedicate this book to efforts to ensure a secure and permanent home for everyone.

Chapter 1

An Introduction to Homelessness and Anthropological Perspectives

As I entered the shelter one evening, I said *"Buenas tardes"* to José, a man with whom I had conversed at another shelter the previous week. José was a tall and thin man in his 40's, who told me that he is HIV+. Last week José said that he believes that the city is letting its buildings deteriorate so that they can tear them down in order to make parking lots for the employees in the insurance companies. Tonight José was especially incensed because his welfare (General Assistance) check was being reduced from $356.00 to $300.00, which means that he is now considered 'employable.' He told me that he plans to die in the tobacco fields, where he worked today. I suggested that he talk with the shelter social worker and call the lawyer handling his disability claim. After showing me the communiqué from welfare, José walked away. About one half an hour later, he fought with another man, and was asked to leave the shelter, which he did. (Glasser 1996: 11)

Homelessness emerged as a public concern in the United States in the late 1970s and early 1980s as Americans began encountering people living on the streets, a way of life which had formerly been confined to the skid rows of large cities. By the mid-1980s to early 1990s, the visibly homeless were becoming a common sight even among those countries with well-developed social safety-net programs, such as Canada. Through television and newspaper reporting, people in North America were also aware of the thousands of people living without adequate housing in African, Asian, and South American countries, though, at least initially, these issues were not connected to homelessness "at home." Much of the early discussion of homelessness in industrialized countries centered on the deinstitutionalization of the mentally ill who were so visible on city streets. By the latter part of the 1980s, however, journalists and social scientists began to consider the tearing down of cheap inner-city housing in the form of old hotels and rooming houses (the process of gentrification) as a major explanation for the lack of housing available to the poorest segment of society. In this way, the public discourse on homelessness in the first world moved away from the pathology model to the lack of housing model, and moved closer to explanations long used in the third world.

As one of the most visible indicators of poverty, homelessness confronts us with our inability to offer everyone the most basic conditions for a healthy and productive life. It leads us to ask what social and political forces could possibly have led to the condition of a group of people meeting their basic needs of shelter, food, and sanitation, on the street, in public view? Grappling with the answers to these questions drives most inquiries about homelessness, including this one.

Defining Homelessness

A widely used and useful conceptualization of homelessness was developed by Peter Rossi (see Rossi et al. 1987: 1336) who distinguishes between the literally homeless (persons who obviously have no access to a conventional dwelling and who would be considered homeless by any conceivable definition of the term) and the precariously or marginally housed (persons with tenuous or very temporary claims to a more or less conventional dwelling or housing). This distinction can be used in studies of the visibly homeless (those in homeless shelters and living on the streets, in encampments, in abandoned buildings, and in places such as subway stations) and the precariously housed (those doubled-up temporarily with other, usually poor, families, or those in inexpensive lodging who pay by the day or week). How widely one casts the "homeless net" has a tremendous impact on the numbers and characteristics of the people included in the definition of homelessness.

Most anthropologists try to use the self-appellation of the group under study. However, in the area of homelessness, this becomes difficult. For example, in the course of their research on housing and homelessness, Watson and Austerberry (1986) interviewed a sample of sixty homeless women in Great Britain about their housing experiences. They asked them, "Do you think of yourself as being homeless?" and "What does the word "homeless" mean to you?"

They found that 30 percent of the women did not think of their present accommodation as their home. Nevertheless, they did not consider themselves homeless. Conversely, the 32 percent who thought of their present accommodation as home did refer to themselves as homeless. The meanings attached to the words "home" and "homeless" were susceptible to shifting understandings of the term, as illustrated by the following words of three different women:

> I really have to confront the whole thing. I look over at the Sally Army hostel [homeless shelter] and think, I'll move in there. What is the difference between me and someone there? It's only an attitude of mind that makes me different from a wino. It doesn't do to dwell on it.

> Homelessness is little old men going around with bags over their shoes. So to that extent I don't think of myself as homeless ... But the only reason I am not actually *homeless* is because the people I'm living with are too middle-class to fling me on the street.

> Homeless? I am in a way. I mean I'm in a hostel – not having a place I could call home. You have to leave this place when you're 60 – so I'm homeless in the sense that it's not for my retirement. (Watson and Austerberry 1986: 103-104)

Added to the difficulty of people's varying definitions of "homeless," is the fact that cultures have different words for the concept, each with different and sometimes subtle connotations. For example, in Montreal, Quebec, people are variously called *les itinérants* by the religious and advocacy community (the newspaper sold on the streets of Montreal is *L'itinéraire*) and *sansabri* (without shelter) for use within professional and academic circles. Some people have suggested that *sans-abri* came into vogue in Montreal *after* the media attention of the United Nations 1987 International Year of Shelter for the Homeless (Glasser, Fournier, and Costopoulos 1996). Cultural differences are also in evidence when homelessness is viewed cross-nationally – one speaks of the *roofless* of India, the *furosha* ("floating people") of Japan, and the *gamino* (street child, from the word "gamin") of Colombia. Different definitions of a home also add to the dilemma of defining homelessness cross-nationally. For example, a person living in a one-room house constructed of mud, sticks, twigs, and branches in a squatter settlement of Nairobi, Kenya (Settlements Information Network Africa, 1986) would be classified as homeless, or at the very least, the housing would be considered marginal in most parts of the industrialized world.

One way to confront this problem is to define homelessness as the opposite of having adequate housing, which can be understood in the following way:

> Adequate, affordable shelter with basic services is a fundamental right of all people. Governments should respect the right of all people to shelter, free from the fear of forced eviction or removal, or the threat of their home being demolished ...

> Adequate shelter includes not only protection from the elements, but also sources of potable water in or close to the house, provision for the removal of household and human liquid and solid wastes, site drainage, emergency life-saving services, and easy access to health care. In urban centers, a house site within easy reach of social and economic opportunities is also an integral part of an adequate shelter. (The Limuru Declaration, as cited in Turner 1988: 187)

An interesting challenge in the effort to define homelessness is the question: when is "no access to a conventional dwelling" *not* homelessness? The answer appears to be when movement from place to place is a part of the *culture* of the group. For example, pastoralists who move with their herds and have no permanent settlement, such as the Kurds of Iraq (Nanda 1991), or hunters and gatherers such as the !Kung of the Kalahari desert (Shostak 1983), or the Travellers (Gypsies) of the United Kingdom (Gmelch 1985; Helleiner 1992 and 1997), would fit this description. So would year-round recreational-vehicle dwellers who do not maintain permanent dwellings anywhere else (Behr and Gober 1982; Counts 1996). On the other hand, James Spradley (1970) demonstrated how men in Seattle's Skid Row make the rounds from jails, treatment centers, inexpensive hotels on Skid Row, and railroad cars, creating a culture that is reminiscent of the seasonal migrations of other nomads.

To further make the point, what would prevent a group of people from *naming* their lack of a permanent home a part of their culture? For example, Susan Hutson (1993), an anthropologist working in Wales, documents the appearance of the New Age Travellers, groups of young people who travel around the United Kingdom in caravans or move into abandoned buildings. Is this an appropriation of the name "Travellers," or is it an accurate description of their culture? Does the group need to have other markers of culture, such as language and common ancestry, in order to warrant membership in a culture, or is a loosely affiliated group, such as men living on the streets, enough?

Finally, should the populations of refugees and immigrants (forced and voluntary transnational migrants), who have long been the subject of anthropological research (see for example, Harrell-Bond and Vourtira 1996, and Brettell 1996a) be included under the rubric "homeless"? Although at first glance the lack of a "homeland" (as in the case of refugees) may appear to be a different topic than life in shelters and on the streets, there is some evidence of overlap. For example, there appear to be a high proportion of refugees in the squatter camps of the Sudan (Bascom 1993) and a high proportion of African immigrants squatting in the vacant HLM's (Habitations de Loyer Modérés, similar to public housing in the United States) in and around Paris (Boudimbou 1992). Therefore, in some cases, being a refugee or immigrant may increase one's vulnerability to various forms of homelessness.

Anthropological Methodology and Analysis of Homelessness

Through the utilization of extended fieldwork, a holistic approach, and cross-cultural perspectives, anthropologists attempt to understand what drives individuals to life on the streets and to shelters, and what prevents them from gaining permanent and secure housing. The periods of extended fieldwork within a culture often result in published ethnographies, which are written descriptions of social and cultural practices. The term ethnography refers to the process of inquiry as well as to the written results of the inquiry. This section offers the reader some examples of how anthropological methods have been applied to the problems associated with homelessness. It also offers some examples of effective advocacy based on anthropological research.

Ethnography, as a hallmark of anthropology, has been developed and refined over the past century (Durrenberger 1996:416-422). At first ethnographic studies were conducted among small, relatively isolated groups of people, although the ethnographic approach is now commonly applied to the study of subcultures within industrialized societies. Ethnography is a way of entering a culture, learning about it, and, as much as possible, communicating a "native" point of view to a wider public. It entails not only noting cultural behaviors and actions, but also understanding *interpretations* of behaviors and beliefs on the part of different members of a society (e.g., how might a homeless woman, a shelter director, a city official, and a community activist view the same situation?). Careful and intensive fieldwork, and a philosophy of cultural relativism, that is, understanding how each element of a culture fits into the larger cultural context without passing moral judgments, form the intellectual underpinnings of anthropological homelessness research today. This depth of understanding, frequently called "thick description" (Ryle 1971 and Geertz 1973), is what makes anthropology's approach to homelessness so valuable. We are "interested sojourners" (Geertz 1973: 20) when we enter the communities of the homeless, and learn about the knowledge that the homeless have acquired and how this knowledge relates to their survival.

The insider's approach attempts to avoid the *a priori* categories of other disciplines, and therefore enables us to see the world through the eyes of the homeless themselves. Anthropological research on homelessness then becomes a good complement to the research of sociologists, psychologists, and public health professionals who often utilize the one-time interview method. Ethnographic studies of groups of homeless people have enabled anthropologists to become advocates by learning, and then presenting, the perspectives of those who are homeless. In such research the relationship between those who are homeless and the researcher is akin to that between teacher and student (Rosenthal 1991: 118). The ethnographic approach has been utilized as a valuable research tool in confronting a wide variety of contemporary problems, including the AIDS crisis (see for example, the work of Singer 1996 and Farmer 1992).

Ethnography allows for exploration of the *meanings* and *interpretations* that people assign to events in their lives, things that are not easily quantifiable. While ethnographic studies can be provocative, accessible, and insightful, they also need to be used with care. The ethnographer, as the prime research instrument, carries biases (e.g., personal, cultural, discipline-bound, class-bound, and gender-bound) which may not always be explicitly acknowledged.

Ethnographic Studies of the Homeless

One of the first contemporary examples of homelessness research was the work of James Spradley (1970). Utilizing participant observation and methods of linguistic anthropology, Spradley was able to document the broad array of adaptive strategies used by men on the streets of Skid Row in Seattle, Washington. He sought to figure out why the men who spent so much time in the "drunk tank" of the local jails, immediately returned to drinking and to the streets upon their release. Spradley was able to closely follow the life of one Skid Row resident, William R. Tanner, a literate man of forty-nine, who was arrested for public drunkenness nine times in the course of the year, and served nearly two hundred days in jail on drunk charges (Spradley 1970:12). At the end of one of his drunk-tank sojourns, Mr. Tanner writes to Spradley, giving him insight into the futility of the drunk tank as a "cure" for alcoholism, and also giving him the title of his book, *You Owe Yourself a Drunk*. Mr. Tanner writes: "I'm gradually trying to introduce myself to society and regain my civilian bearings. If you can trail me along this devious track, you've a much better acumen than I. After thirty days in jail you owe yourself a drunk" (Spradley 1970:26).

Twenty years after Spradley's work, in California, geographer Jennifer Wolch and anthropologist Stacy Rowe studied the adaptation of women and men who were living on the beaches and in the encampments, streets, and shelters of Los Angeles, utilizing the architecture of modern life for their survival out-of-doors (Wolch and Rowe 1992). For example, in their quest for a place to sleep, one group of friends on occasion used beach lockers:

> Lockers are another key item shared by St. Mary's [drop-in center and restaurant for the homeless] clients. Not only are clothes and other belongings stored there, but lockers are large enough for a person to crawl into and snooze. As Dee describes it, "both me and Mike and his friend, we all squeeze in there and we go to sleep ... It's snug. We're all close together; we're all warm; we've got a lot of blankets. We do okay." (Wolch and Rowe 1992: 125)

Anthropologists have frequently documented the kinds of mutual support networks developed by the homeless. Rather than places of chaos, there is a sense of community created in places like soup kitchens and homeless shelters. In one ethnography of a soup kitchen (Glasser 1988) various individuals provided leadership in the form of information and support to the rest of the guests:

From his seat near the coffee pot in the dining room, and his piece of sidewalk outside the Hotel Paradise, Pedro was a source of friendship and help to the other Puerto Rican men and women who came to Middle City. He let the newly arrived people know where to get welfare, food stamps, and clothes. He greeted people as they entered the dining room, and he was friendly with the soup kitchen volunteers.

Pedro had an affectionate relationship with many of the children in the soup kitchen. Sometimes, when one of the children was crying, he would walk over, pick up the crying child and soothe him. Pedro was friends with Marie Gamache [another central figure of the soup kitchen]. When she entered the soup kitchen, he often greeted her with "Hey, let me buy you a cup of coffee and a donut" [a soup kitchen joke]. To this Marie laughed and said, "*No, mucho gordo.*" (Glasser 1988: 111)

Utilizing Holism

Holism in anthropology refers to the fact that within a cultural setting, *everything* is considered relevant to study. Anthropologists ideally should be able to understand all aspects of the human condition, including the biological, cultural, social, linguistic, and psychological spheres of life (Bodley 1996). Two of the founders of anthropology, Bronislaw Malinowski and Franz Boas, made use of the holistic approach by attempting to grapple with many different elements of culture. For example, in trying to understand the workings of exchange networks among the Trobiand Islanders of Papua New Guinea, Malinowski considered styles of canoe construction, roles of magic, and social stratification. Similarly, Boas considered property and potlatching (ritual feasts and exchanges) in understanding marriage among the Kwatkuitl of Northwest America (Borofsky 1994:13).

The research of Janet Fitchen (1991a, 1991b) regarding rural homelessness provides a good example of the holistic approach to understanding the causes of homelessness. Working in rural New York State, Fitchen documented the constellation of forces that may push rural people into homelessness.

One underlying cause for rural homelessness is an increase in rural poverty. Manufacturing jobs that sustained communities through factory work have left the Northeast. Some of the urban poor have moved to the country in search of more hospitable environments. Fitchen documented the tax incentives that make second (vacation) home ownership by the middle class advantageous, at the expense of inflating the cost of rural housing. Added to these factors is the tightening of zoning and housing regulations which keep people from living in some low-income houses and trailers, again pushing them into the rental market. Now even the doubling-up of families, the informal source of help for many of the rural poor (should a son or daughter lose their housing, they could always come home) is much more difficult (or impossible) in a rented apartment.

> Traditionally, open-country poor people have had the security and limited cash expense of owning a place to live, or having parents or other relatives who owned a place, even if it was just a crumbling farmhouse, a tarpaper-sided shack, or an old trailer encased in wooden additions. It did not matter so much what one owned, but that one owned it. (Fitchen 1991b: 195)

Much of rural homelessness takes the form of frequent moves from one unaffordable rent to another, occasionally interspersed with time in a motel or shelter. On a household level, the rise in single-parent families and stepfamilies is intertwined with a loss of access to housing. For example, Fitchen traced the early departure of many teenagers from their parental home to the occasion of the mother or father's remarriage.

Though rarely explicitly articulated, the theoretical construct that has guided a large part of the anthropological research on homelessness, and one that is conducive to the holistic perspective, has been the ecological model. The ecological perspective looks at all of the material constraints imposed on a group of people and their adaptations to them (Godelier 1994; Rappaport 1994). Anthropologists have studied the loss of affordable housing, the loss of manufacturing jobs in the cities, the reduction or elimination of financial assistance, and racial discrimination in employment and housing as major contributors to the conditions that lead to a lack of housing for the most vulnerable populations. Whereas those working in other disciplines such as psychology, sociology, and public health have shared the tendency, at least initially, to view homelessness from the "personal pathology" perspective (i.e., explanations that center on issues of an individual's mental illness, alcoholism, and drug addiction), many anthropologists have framed the condition of homelessness within broad social and cultural contexts. The most successful studies have looked at every possible factor that contributes to the state of homelessness, whether it is internally (personally) or externally (structurally) induced.

Cross-Cultural Perspectives

Anthropology has, from its beginnings, focused on the study of cultures unfamiliar to the anthropologist, and it is only within the last several decades that anthropologists have turned their attention to domestic issues. Yet cross-cultural perspectives continue to be of value in that they entail a degree of detachment difficult to achieve in one's own culture (Bodley 1996: 10). When anthropologists have viewed homelessness cross-culturally (e.g., Glasser 1994), they have discussed homelessness as a construct that varies greatly from culture to culture. Below is an overview of some of the conceptualizations of homelessness that occur elsewhere in the world. Note that in countries such as India, the term for people living outside, without shelter is *roofless*, a term that does not imply the social pathology perspective so often associated with the word *home-less*. Developing countries tend to discuss the issue of lack of adequate housing from the point of view of rural-to-urban migration. For Western nations, homelessness historically has been linked to alcoholism (e.g., the skid rows of major cities). In the latter part of the twentieth century, homelessness was tied to widespread substance abuse and the deinstitutionalization of the mentally ill, coupled with the gentrification of the cities and a decrease in governmental support for social housing.

The industry and inventiveness of people in various parts of the world to create their own housing out of found materials has been documented. For example, Peter Lloyd (1980), a

Table 1.1 International Conceptualizations of Homelessness

Lack of shelter

roofless (India)
sin techo (Latin America)
sans-abri (France; Quebec, Canada)
sleeping rough (United Kingdom)
without permanent address, *sans adresse fixe* (generic, United Nations term)

Cutoff from a household or other people

clochard (tramp, France)
pennebruder (men who share sleeping quarters and prison brothers, Germany)
desamparado (without protection or comfort from other people, Latin America)
furosha (floating people, Japan)
tuna wisma, orang gelandangan (uneducated, poor, suspected of crime, Indonesia)
puliukko (elderly male alcoholic who sleeps under bridges, Finland)

Homeless, street children

gamino (Colombia)
pivete or *pixote* (street child involved in crime, *pixote* is from the movie *Pixote*, Brazil)
khate (rag picker, Kathmandu, Nepal)
parking boy (from common job in informal economy, Nairobi, Kenya)

Squatter settlements, spontaneous settlements

bidonvilles (tin cities, Francophone Africa, France)
pueblos jóvenes (young towns, Lima, Peru)
mong liu, nong min gong (former peasants who move into the city illegally, China)
favelas (Brazil)
squats (England)
kampung (village, Indonesia)

Commonly linked associations with homelessness in North America

* rural-to-urban migration
* chronic alcoholism or substance abuse
* deinstitutionalization of the mentally ill
* gentrification, decreased government support for social housing, service economy

(Adapted from *Homelessness in Global Perspective,* 1994.)

British anthropologist, argued that rather than being squatter settlements of despair, the self-made houses of the *sin techo* (roofless) poor on the periphery of Lima, Peru, were in fact the beginning of stable housing with the potential for vital communities, and were being called *pueblos jóvenes* (young towns) in order to reflect that reality. The idea of self-made housing as one response to homelessness has been tried in many North American cities, including New York, Philadelphia, and Toronto, and at times, anthropologists have been involved in these efforts.

Advocacy

Despite the many fine ethnographic works on homelessness, Kim Hopper has warned that anthropologists are in danger of only adding "local color" to the larger discussions of homelessness, without being able to really effect any changes in public understanding or policies regarding the homeless (Hopper 1995). There have been studies, however, that have indeed made an impact on social policy, through their careful documentation of formerly "hidden" populations and through their holistic analysis.

For example, over the past fifteen years Anna Lou Dehavenon (1995) has been documenting the conditions of poverty in New York City, and implicating the lack of affordable housing, low welfare payments, and a slow welfare bureaucracy in the increase of families who are homeless. Recently she documented how the city's emergency assistance units worsen health conditions among homeless families as they wait for an assignment to a shelter or to housing. Camping out on plastic chairs with poor food, lack of ventilation, and lack of ability to rest leads to illness for these vulnerable families. She has also demonstrated the difficulties of living doubled-up in another family's apartment, which is the arrangement frequently encountered among the very poor of New York City. One of the interesting things about Dehavenon's research is her presentation of it. Her press conferences, news releases, and communiqués to city and state politicians all have helped her recommendations to be taken seriously (Dehavenon 1994).

Janet Fitchen was able to use her holistic approach in speaking to state and federal legislators on behalf of the rural poor (Fitchen 1994). She helped the legislators see that homelessness was not just a big-city phenomenon but was a condition faced by rural residents as well. She highlighted the independence and fortitude of the rural poor, who are often shunted into a more dependent and passive role as poor renters unless social policies are formulated with them in mind. Since many poor rural people own their own houses, Fitchen outlined recommendations that supported home ownership. For example, she documented how trailer parks that are about to be closed may be turned into cooperatives by their tenants (Fitchen 1996:13). In general, she used what she knew about the culture of rural poverty to make social policy recommendations to prevent homelessness.

The careful ethnographic study of the homeless in New York by Ellen Baxter and Kim Hopper (1981) demonstrated that many of the people living on the streets were not deranged, but were in fact making rational decisions about where to sleep based on their own safety (conditions at many of the shelters were violent). Hopper's research findings (and field notes) were subpoenaed in court in a class-action lawsuit that had been filed on behalf of homeless men. The ethnographic record impressed the judge:

> Confronted with several photographs of toilets smeared with fecal matter, for example, the judge remarked noting the obvious filth – which, after all, could have been staged – but on the fact that the commodes had neither seats nor partitions between them. (Hopper 1990:111)

Hopper's testimony, based on his ethnographic research, became the basis for a court decision which had the effect of improving the safety and hygiene of New York City shelters.

Some of the best work on homelessness is that which is capable of communicating the experience of homelessness to others, as well as that which points the way to promising initiatives to secure permanent housing. In the chapters that follow, we will present findings from our own research and from those of other scholars that deepen our understanding of contemporary homelessness.

Chapter 2

Patterns of Homelessness

Who are the homeless? This basic question must be answered before meaningful social policy can be introduced to combat homelessness. The hope is that if one can identify which groups of people tend to be homeless, then one can either construct programs that prevent homelessness or tailor services for the people who are without shelter. For example, in a study of the homeless of Hartford, Connecticut, Glasser (1996) found that there was a group of men coming directly out of prison and going into the city-run McKinney Shelter. These men then were spending a greater length of time in the shelter (more than three months) than the rest of the residents. In response to this emerging pattern, the Connecticut Prison Association, a service organization for newly released inmates, began to devote much of their work to finding appropriate housing for newly released former prisoners (Walter 1998). Glasser also found a group of older (for the shelter population, over fifty years old) long-term residents of Mckinney Shelter. Forcing them to leave the shelter to find their own apartments did not seem realistic, so another agency, South Park Inn, developed long-term housing for the frail, older long-term shelter residents (Walter 1998), again, in response to the demographic patterns of the homeless emerging in the shelters.

Illustration 2.1 Abandoned building in Hartford, Connecticut, site of squatters (Original work by Jason Glasser)

One of the difficulties of discovering patterns of homelessness is simply how we define and enumerate the homeless. For example, if we study those who end up in homeless shelters, are we studying the extent of *services* for the homeless or are we studying the phenomenon itself? If many communities are more comfortable in providing services for homeless families (who are least affected by mental illness and substance use and abuse) than for single people, are we really correct in concluding that a large proportion of the homeless are living in families? Do we view staying with friends and family on a very temporary basis ("crashing") as a category of homelessness, or as a *risk* factor in the creation of homelessness? We have witnessed many times that the way in which homelessness is defined has a great impact on the establishment of priorities in funding services for the homeless.

When we look at the patterns of homelessness we must also be aware that some of the "characteristics" we assign to the people may in fact be induced by their homeless state, rather than being a contributing factor to it. If, for example, we find a higher percentage of people in some state of homelessness reporting greater stress or depression than in the rest of the population, we must ask if this is a characteristic they had *before* they lost their housing (and thus may have contributed to the process), or if is this an outgrowth of living on the street or in shelters. Similarly, is poor nutrition or poor health a precursor of homelessness, or is it a natural outcome of eating at shelters and soup kitchens (or not eating at all) and inconsistent health care?

Despite these definitional and methodological problems, there is a wealth of research that describes the patterns of homelessness. The latest generation of studies attempts to capture the episodic nature of homelessness, with frequent exits from and returns to various states of shelter. Where possible, studies have contrasted the poor-but-housed population with the homeless, trying to discern what factors "protect" the poor person from falling into homelessness. The following section will provide an overview of some of the best research available regarding patterns of homelessness.

Homeless Men

The classic case of homelessness is the lone, unattached male. He is either viewed with fear and revulsion (his lack of connection to kith or kin linked to both a lack of control and a sense of responsibility), or he is viewed more positively as the romantic "traveling man" of Depression-era fame, who has given up his attachment to the material world of schedules and obligations (Glasser 1994:14). Historically, homeless men were often assumed to be inhabitants of the skid rows of U.S. cities, which were usually neighborhoods containing cheap lodging for transient and marginally employed (and sometimes alcoholic) men. The term comes from the Skid Row (so named in reference to logs skidding down the road) of Seattle, Washington, where cheap rooms were available to lumberjacks in the early twentieth century (Cohen and Sokolovsky 1989:50). Much of the single-room-occupancy housing in skid rows has been torn down in the urban renewal programs of the 1960s and 1970s, and in the process of gentrification of the 1980s and 1990s. The irony here is that *having access to an inexpensive room with a key* in a convenient location, and in the company of other single men (i.e., very much like the old skid row), is the ideal to which many of the most innovative supportive housing programs for the homeless now aspire.

In a 1987 study of randomly selected shelter and homeless soup kitchen users in the U.S., Martha Burt (1992:14-15) found that 80 percent of the homeless people were men and most of the men (73 percent) were alone. In terms of demographic characteristics, single homeless men were White (48 percent), Black (40 percent), and Hispanic (9 percent), were never married (57 percent), and were between the ages of 25 and 44 (57 percent). They had been homeless for an average of forty-one months in contrast to thirty-three months for single women and sixteen months for women with children, respectively (Burt 1992:18). Single men had a 37 percent rate of inpatient treatment for chemical dependence and a 19 percent rate of hospitalization for mental illness. In terms of incarceration, 60 percent of the men had spent time in jail, and 29 percent had spent time in prison (Burt 1992:22). The picture that emerges of homeless

Illustration 2.2 Homeless man (Original work by Jason Glasser)

men is of a seriously troubled group of people who, in contrast to women, are in the state of homelessness for the longest period of time. Although not perhaps winning the most sympathy from the public, the single man constitutes the majority of the homeless population.

Homeless Women

In contrast to homeless men, homeless women garnered little attention in the literature until the 1980s, in part because their numbers were small and in part because a characteristic survival strategy of homeless women is to keep hidden from view (Glasser 1994:39). The work of Joanne Passaro in New York City (1996) also corroborates the degree to which men are highly visible in public space, and women are not. In this section, we will focus on homeless *single* women, who, although they may be mothers, do *not* have their children with them. The term "single" here encompasses a wide variety of situations and reflects a wide array of needs. Single may include women who have never been married, young women without children, women whose children are living in foster homes or with other family members, elderly women, heterosexual women, and lesbian women.

In the 1987 national study referred to previously, Martha Burt (1992:14-15) found that 9 percent of the homeless people were single women, and another 9 percent were women accompanied by their children. Single women were Black (47 percent), White (40 percent) and Hispanic (7 percent), were never married (49 percent), and were between the ages of twenty-five and forty-four (53 percent). They had been homeless a shorter time than men, with a mean of thirty-three months (Burt 1992:18). Women's rate of hospitalization for mental illness was higher than that of men (27 percent), although their rate of inpatient treatment for chemical dependence was lower (19 percent). Their rate of incarceration (32 percent had spent time in jail and 2 percent had spent time in prison) was significantly less than the rate for men (Burt 1992:22). A study of female veterans treated by the Homeless Chronically Mentally Ill Veterans Program also found a larger proportion of the homeless female veterans had a major psychiatric disorder and a lesser rate of substance-use diagnoses than the male group (Leda, Rosenheck, and Gallup 1992). The implication for programs targeting homeless single women is that there should be substantial mental health help included.

Homeless Families

Homeless families (i.e., homeless households that include at least one adult with at least one child under age eighteen) have received much attention in large part because the presence of children among the homeless confronts us most directly with society's failure to guarantee a minimum standard of protection. The questions of who these families are, how they became homeless, and how we may prevent and ameliorate their homelessness carry a certain urgency with them.

In an article reviewing eleven studies of homeless families (each study included at least fifty families) by Kay Young McChesney (1995), there were eight risk factors that appeared to increase the likelihood that poor families would become homeless. These risk factors were the following: single mother as head of household, being African American, young age of the head of household, substance abuse by mother or her male partner, childhood victimization of mother, adult victimization (e.g., battered), pregnancy or recent childbirth, and lack of (or having exhausted) social support, particularly housing support (McChesney 1995: 441). Risk factors did not include a psychiatric disability nor arrest record or incarceration. McChesney hypothesizes that the risk factors work to make the family especially vulnerable to being forced to leave their housing, which then forces them to face the structural factors of too few affordable units for poor families, which then makes them homeless.

Ellen Bassuk and John Buchner (1997) contrast a sample of single mothers and their children living in shelters in Worcester, Massachusetts, with a sample of low-income single mothers who were *never* homeless. In this way the risk factors and the protective factors of family homelessness become evident. When the homeless families were compared to the poor-but-housed families, it was found that the mothers of the homeless families were more likely to have been in foster-care placement and to have had a female caregiver who used drugs. In their adult lives they had lived in the area for a shorter period of time. They were also more likely to be African American or Puerto Rican. Factors that prevented homelessness for the poor families were linked with the mother's being a primary tenant (her name was on the lease), receiving monetary housing subsidies, and having a larger social network.

Both of the above studies of homeless families underline the importance of housing supports that *prevent* the loss of housing for families. These supports could be in the form of increased scattered-site, affordable housing owned and operated by non-profit community organizations, rent supplements to offset the large proportion of income devoted to paying for housing, and eviction-prevention programs. An example of the latter is the Tenancy Settlement/Mediation Program of Passaic, New Jersey (Cucio 1992). Here mediation is offered that seeks to restore the tenant-landlord relationship in cases of tenant-landlord disputes. In 1990 approximately 1,300 tenancy disputes, representing 3,600 adults and children, were successfully settled.

Homeless Youth

A visit to many cities of North America will reveal a highly visible scene of youth on the street. For example, "squeegee kids" hang out street corners and wash motorists' car windows for small change. Street youth may be sleeping in abandoned buildings, "crashing" for the night in a friend's place, or staying in a youth shelter, and yet there are few studies that focus on them. The following two studies offer a beginning look at youth homelessness.

In a study of homeless youth in Hollywood, California, by Robertson, Koegel, and Ferguson (1989), ninety-three young people were interviewed, utilizing standardized measurements.

The sample was drawn from youth in shelters, meal programs, drop-in centers, abandoned buildings, parks, fast-food restaurants, and street corners. The researchers defined homeless youth as individuals age seventeen or younger who had spent the previous night in a formal shelter, in an "improvised shelter" (e.g., abandoned buildings, vehicles, public places), or "on the streets" (e.g., parks, beaches, or walking around) (p. 420). Overall they found that the majority of the group were male (61.3 percent) and white (60.2 percent), and that a majority (52.3 percent) had moved into Los Angeles County during the previous six months. Most had been homeless more than once, and their total time as homeless averaged over six months. Most of the sample was from the "street," and only 15.7 percent identified shelters as their usual place to sleep.

In a study from Wales, Susan Hutson and Mark Liddiard (1991) charted the "homeless careers" of 115 youth who had been evicted from their homes or had had to leave foster care. The researchers found that some options, such as staying with friends or returning home, became less and less viable as the months on the road wore on. Further, "sleeping rough" (sleeping outside) and squatting in abandoned buildings became a more frequent option the longer the youth was homeless.

There is a great need for further research regarding homeless youth. Among the important questions are how youth become homeless, what is the likelihood of a homeless youth becoming a homeless adult, and, most important, what types of services and interventions help homeless youth become housed and stay housed?

Homeless Children

When we turn to the question of homeless children in North America, there is relatively little written, and the studies that do exist refer primarily to children living with their parents in shelters. In the developing world, particularly in Latin America and South Asia, literature on (and community work for) street children abounds (Glasser 1994:53). A widely used typology that describes homeless children in developing countries is children *on* the streets (those who work on the streets during the day, but return home most nights), and children *of* the streets (those children who work *and* sleep on the streets and have minimal family contact) (UNICEF 1986). Much of the literature from street schools and health clinics for homeless children focuses on how to distinguish between the two groups, in order to provide help that will prevent the child on the street from losing all contact and support from his or her family. Supporting the poor family before they abandon some of their children to the street is the priority in terms of prevention. Once children live on the street full-time, the most innovative programs support the children's independence, and usually concentrate on helping them survive economically (and within the law) and on providing some basic health care and education, all within the street milieu (Glasser 1994:80).

In North America one useful study that focuses on the needs of homeless children includes a statewide survey of homeless children in New Hampshire (Nord and Luloff 1995). This study estimated that 34 percent of the 14,415 homeless in New Hampshire in 1988 were children. In-depth interviews were conducted with twenty homeless youth and children, and their families. The researchers also talked to school and community workers about the needs of homeless children. They found that the causes for homelessness among the single-parent families centered on family disruption (divorce, separation, and domestic violence), whereas the two-parent families had experienced an economic crisis (e.g., loss of a job). Whatever the cause, once homeless, children were found to be tired, experiencing an inability to concentrate, having difficulty academically and socially, and subject to frequent changes of schools and out-of-school periods. The authors emphasize that these problems occurred during the entire residential crisis period, as the family was moving through a cycle of lost housing, shelters, and attempts to stay with family and friends. An interesting finding was that New Hampshire schools often closed their eyes to the paperwork required for school entrance (which can take time) in an effort to minimize further loss of school experience.

Mental Illness

For many people in North America the issue of homelessness is closely tied to the phenomenon of *deinstitutionalization*, which refers to the process of having people who were hospitalized with psychiatric problems leave the hospital in order to live in the community. In the United States and Canada, the movement away from long-term hospital stays in favor of short-term, crisis-oriented hospitalizations and then community placements occurred in force during the 1960s and 1970s. Life in the community was considered more humane than life in the large psychiatric institutions. However, approximately ten years after the community placements began there appeared to be a visible segment of the former patients who were roaming the streets, muttering to themselves, and generally not being cared for by "the community." The early placements in group homes, boarding houses, and apartments fell into disarray (or were tenuous at best in the first place). The former patients wandered away from the placements, and many stopped taking their medications. How many of the homeless population really are mentally ill became an object of great interest in the research community and in the general public.

When rates of mental illness among the homeless are contrasted with rates in the general population, we find that most studies with good methodology report that 20 to 50 percent of the homeless population in the U.S. suffer from severe mental illness (i.e., schizophrenia, major affective disorders, paranoia and other psychoses, and personality disorders) in contrast to 1 percent in the general population (Burt 1992:108-109). Although much attention has been given to the effect of the deinstitutionalization of the mentally ill on rates of homelessness, researchers were reporting a 20-percent rate of severe mental illness among skid row residents even in the 1950s, before the era of returning the hospitalized mentally ill to the community (Burt 1992:109).

An interesting study from England looked at which type of homeless mentally ill who were served by health clinics (which also provided help with housing and financial assistance) were most likely to lose contact with the agency (Marshall et al.

1994). In a follow-up study of seventy-one patients, 43 percent had lost contact with the clinic. The loss of contact was strongly associated with the homeless mentally ill who were dually diagnosed as having a substance abuse problem, which the authors think resulted in their loss of housing. This is the kind of research that can help tailor services to specific subgroups within a service center.

Substance Abuse

There is substantial evidence that alcoholism is the most pervasive health problem of the homeless in the United States (see an excellent review by Fischer and Breakey 1991). The rate of alcohol abuse has been estimated to be 58 to 68 percent for homeless men; 30 percent for homeless single women; and 10 percent for mothers in homeless families. In the general population the rates for alcohol abuse are estimated to be 10 percent for men and between 3 and 5 percent for women (Fischer and Breakey 1991:1118). Alcohol abuse rates among the homeless also vary by ethnicity, with the prevalence for Whites (57.1 percent) being significantly higher than for Nonwhites (34.2 percent) (Robertson, Koegel, and Ferguson 1989).

Determining the rate of drug use among the homeless has been especially fraught with problems, since many studies do not distinguish between drug and alcohol use or between occasional use and a regular drug habit. An estimated rate of between 25 and 50 percent of the homeless population use illicit drugs, and this exceeds the rate of the general population in the U.S. (Fischer and Breakey 1991:1120).

In their study of homeless youth in Hollywood, California, Robertson, Koegel, and Ferguson (1989) found that almost half (48.4 percent) of their respondents could be diagnosed as being either alcohol users or being alcohol dependent at some point in their lives, and that even the non-abusers drank and were at high risk of becoming problem drinkers. The authors found that being on the street exacerbated the amount of drinking. Interestingly, very few of the total sample (6.5 percent) said that their drinking was a contributing factor to their homelessness, although almost one quarter (23.7 percent) said that alcohol-related problems (including alcohol-induced violence) had led to their leaving home. Very few of the youth had had any kind of alcohol treatment.

Most of the youth of this study were preoccupied with survival needs: having adequate food, shelter, and clothing. Robertson, Koegel, and Ferguson strongly advocate that treatment for alcohol and drugs be offered along with material help. An interesting observation from this study is that the alcohol users were less likely to utilize shelters than the nonusers were (probably due at least in part to the restrictive policies of the shelters). This is a cause for concern since not using shelters often puts the alcohol-using homeless youth beyond of the reach of help.

In an excellent study examining the *overlap* of mental health and substance abuse problems among the homeless, 1260 shelter residents in New York City were interviewed, utilizing a fifty-seven-page interview protocol (Struening and Padgett 1990). How, the researchers asked, is health status related to the individual's involvement with alcohol, drugs, mental disorder, and a combination of all three? This study population was generally described as young, male, minority, never married, and relatively well educated (most had finished high school). It is not surprising that the coexistence of heavy substance use with symptoms (or a history) of mental disorder resulted in very high rates of poor health, disability, and worsening health conditions. The often-cited health problems were hypertension, stomach and liver problems, and respiratory disease. The implication of this study is again that medical and mental-health care (including substance-abuse treatment) need to be integrated with services for the homeless. Especially important is early and effective intervention with substance abusers in order to circumvent a lifetime of health consequences from alcohol and/or drug abuse (Struening and Padgett 1990:79).

Beyond the epidemiology of substance use among the alcohol and drug-using homeless population, Kim Hopper (1990) argues that providing housing is a first step in rehabilitation. Given the episodic nature of homelessness for many of the population, it is also important to consider providing adequate support to individuals during their *housed* periods. Later we will turn to the topic of supportive housing as one of the remedies for homelessness.

Counting the Homeless

An interesting corollary to describing the homeless is determining their numbers. In fact, one of the first questions raised in the public consciousness about the homeless was how many homeless there are. If we can see people emerging from abandoned buildings and subway tunnels in the early hours of the morning, how many more people must there be hidden from sight?

In many countries of the world, the decennial census represents the most complete attempt to count the population within their borders. Because the methodology is usually based on the *household* or domicile (where people sleep), there has often been a systematic omission of the homeless. In the United States there has been a drive to remedy this undercount (as it is called) of the homeless since the 1970s. In this effort, the tools of anthropology have been utilized in the search for accurate and culturally congruent methodologies.

In an essay recounting the history of anthropology and the U.S. Bureau of the Census, Cathy Hines (1985) suggests that an impetus for employing anthropologists at the Census Bureau was that, for almost fifty years, evaluations of the decennial counts indicated that there were some *groups of people* who were likely to be missed. Anthropologists were employed, in large part, because of their expertise in participant observation which could be utilized to enter the communities of the undercounted.

In the 1970s, Peter C. Hainer discovered major sources of "working misunderstandings" (a phrase coined by Paul Bohannan, in reference to dominant and subordinate groups in colonial Africa) that resulted in representations of urban African-American households that were not truly reflective of reality, but rather reflected a socially constructed reality *created* by the Census Bureau itself. Hainer had the opportunity, through participant observation, to observe census-takers, who were themselves community members, working with households in an urban African-American neighborhood, literally *creating* household relationships for the purpose of the census forms.

In four kinship-household charts (see below), Hainer presents the same constellation of people, whose relationships are presented for four different purposes. The social family includes all of the people who interact daily and share resources for food, clothing, sleeping, and (very important) child-rearing; biological relationships indicate biological kinship; the "where people sleep/where children are kept" constellation presents six separate addresses for people of one exchange network; and finally, the "official" relationships show three AFDC (Aid to Families with Dependent Children) households, one General Assistance household, one Supplemental Security Income household, and two households not receiving any assistance. The latter was the household configuration that both the enumerators and the social family itself tried to present for the census, since, despite assurances of confidentiality, there was a desire for the census form to be consistent with the "official" view of the relationships.

Figure 2.1 Same People – Different Definitions

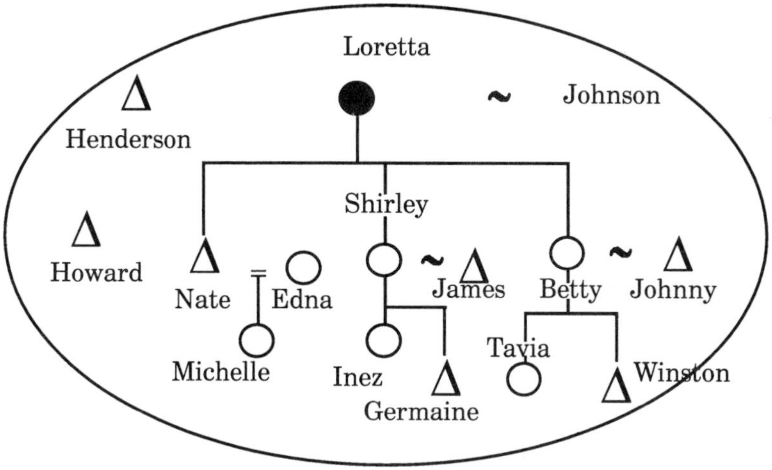

A. Social Family Relationships: Everyone here included. This is an exchange network. People here interact daily and share resources (mostly money, food, and clothes).

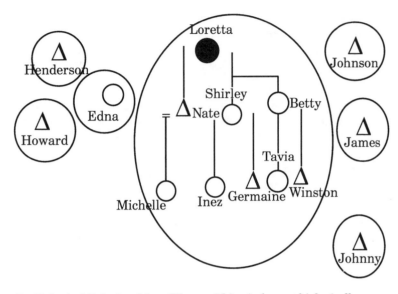

B. Biological Relationships: (Those within circles are biologically related).

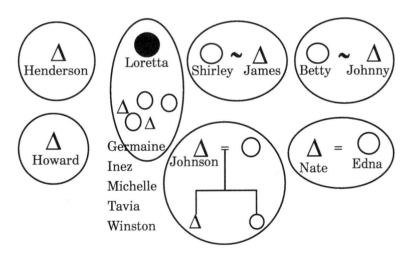

C. Where People Sleep/Where Children are Kept. (Circles here indicate separate addresses. N.B.: All these people "live" within a few blocks of each other, often in the same building, and move together as a unit.)

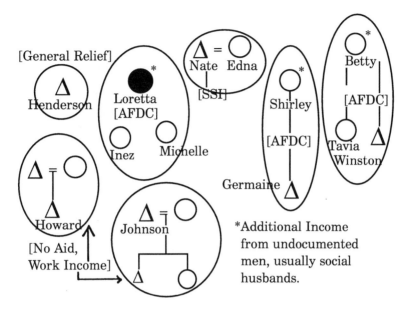

D. "Official" Relationships: – Welfare, Schools, Courts, Census: Source of Income.

(Charts developed by Peter C. Hainer)

Both the census-takers and the households themselves in Hainer's participant observations said to each other, "What are we going to do about all of these men?" (1985: 7) and in fact, it is not difficult to understand how only the public assistance and mostly male-less networks would be included in the census-takers' charts. The non-assisted men, who are actually an integral part of the social family, are "lost" to officialdom.

In another study of undercounting in the inner city, Margaret Boone (1987), an anthropologist who worked with the Census Bureau in the 1980s matched a sample of enumerated households in Washington D.C. in 1983-1984 with a sample of households where a female member had given birth to a low-weight infant. Because of the depth of information known from the low-birth weight study, Boone evaluated the census study in terms of the people and the households most likely to be missed.

Boone concludes that men are the people *within* a household most likely to be missed, thereby corroborating the findings of Hainer. However, in addition Boone found a serious undercount of African-American women and children. The most "reachable" *households* were those that *did* include an adult male, perhaps reflecting a greater degree of residential stability. Boone recommends increasing public awareness about the value of cooperating with the census among inner-city African-American neighborhoods in order to underline the importance of political representation and neighborhood funding, which is tied, at least in part, to the census figures.

Anthropologists were instrumental in the development and implementation of the homeless count in the 1990 U.S. decennial census, which attempted to include the *literally homeless* (those living outside and in shelters) in the total U.S. population. Leslie Brownrigg and Matt T. Salo, both anthropologists, initiated and supervised a number of ethnographic studies which tried to assess the relative accuracy of the homeless count, and to recommend new strategies for subsequent censuses.

In the United States, a systematic effort to count the homeless occurred on March 20, 1990, during S-Night (for shelter and street), eleven days before the regular April 1 household count. The Census Bureau instructions for S-Night were:

> First, we will conduct one special operation ("shelter and street night") on March 20, 1990 to count persons in *pre-identified* emergency shelters (public and private) and open locations in the streets or other places not intended for habitation. This special operation includes all hotels/motels costing $12 or less per night, hotels/motels used entirely to shelter the homeless (regardless of cost), and pre-identified rooms in hotels/motels used for homeless persons and families. Enumeration will occur when the population is generally settled for the night. For shelters, enumeration will usually occur from 6 p.m. to midnight; street enumeration, from 2 a.m. to 4 a.m. (U.S. Department of Commerce, Bureau of the Census 1990b)

Further instructions to the enumerators included not waking up sleeping people, but only noting their race, gender, and approximate age; not entering abandoned buildings, but waiting outside these buildings from 4 a.m. to 8 a.m. to meet the people who had been sleeping inside; not counting people on the street who were in uniform (such as police) or who were obviously engaged in money-making activities (by which was meant drug-dealing and prostitution); but including people involved in begging and panhandling who were at a pre-identified place. It was stressed that the census-takers not try to make judgments about who was homeless and who was not, but to count *everyone* in the places that had been identified by the local municipality or county as sites where the homeless could be found at night. The Bureau of the Census knew that they would not be able to include the homeless who were well hidden, moving about, or in other than the pre-identified locations with this methodology. There was a separate count for women in shelters for domestic violence, as well as for those people who had "no usual home elsewhere" (this is the official phrase) and who resided in halfway houses, maternity homes, agricultural workers' dormitories, commercial campgrounds, and other non-household living situations.

The final numbers, released by the Bureau of the Census, of homeless people in the 1990 census was 178,638 for persons in emergency shelters, and 49,734 for persons visible at pre-identified street locations (U.S. Department of Commerce, Bureau of the Census 1990a). The total of 228,372 was closer to the HUD (Department of Housing and Urban Development) estimate of between 250,000 and 350,000 homeless people in 1984 but considerably below the two to three million presented by advocacy groups throughout the 1980s (Wright and Devine 1992). The total U.S. population reported for 1990 was 248,709,873 (U.S. Department of Commerce, Bureau of the Census 1992).

How well did the Census Bureau do on this homeless enumeration? By most accounts, the shelter count was reasonably accurate. However, the evaluation of the street count was that there continued to be an undercount of the non-sheltered literally homeless. To assess the accuracy of the street count, Kim Hopper had suggested the use of "decoys," census observers who would be deployed in areas that had been determined to be congregating spots for the homeless. These decoys would be expected to be counted as homeless (and therefore appear in the S-Night enumeration). They could also actively *observe* the census operation. Their census form would later be removed from the final count. According to a thorough review of the decoy operation, the "hit-rate" (i.e., the proportion of the decoys counted) in the five cities of this evaluation ranged from 22 percent to 66 percent (Wright and Devine 1992:361). Therefore, in even the best cases, the counting effort missed about one third of the street homeless population.[1]

The most common problems were that the enumerators did not show up at almost half of the sites and that there was a lack of follow-through in interviewing occupants of the sites. Monitors noted that most of the time the enumerators just filled out the forms based on their observations. When they did approach site occupants, they questioned the person as to whether or not he was homeless (in contradiction to the Census Bureau's instructions). In general, the census enumerators were hastily trained, had some trouble locating the sites, and appeared fearful of approaching the occupants of these pre-designated spots.

While preparing and carrying out the 1990 homeless count, anthropologists were also engaged in developing a daytime strategy for conducting a homeless census at service centers such as soup kitchens (called the S-Day count). In this daytime count, enumerators would be able to interview people when they were awake, and in more depth than could possibly be accomplished in the dead of night. It was also safer for both the enumerator and the enumerated. Further, those who were doubled up with other families (the "precariously housed," to use Rossi's term) could also be interviewed.

Matt T. Salo and Pamela Campanelli (1991) utilized ethnographic methods in the city of Baltimore in order to canvass those service centers where homeless people routinely meet their needs for food, clothing, and medical assistance. In casting this much wider net to the service centers, however, it was inevitable that they would meet poor but housed people as well. Therefore, some brief screening questions needed to be developed in order to count only homeless clients. Due to time and money constraints, the daytime strategy was confined to homeless men.

The team of Salo and Campanelli (1991:133) observed and talked with homeless men in Washington, D.C, and Baltimore in fast-food outlets, plasma banks, day-labor agencies, parks, alleys, empty lots, underpasses, soup kitchens, and social service agency waiting rooms – in other words, all the places where one might encounter homeless men. The researchers found that the best places to find the most homeless people were soup kitchens and some other daytime services, and that the best time was on a weekday at the end of the month, when check money had all been spent. Questions asked included detailed inquiries regarding sleeping quarters, demographic questions (these were also used to weed out duplicated interviews, since there is typically much movement among service centers), and questions about occupation or skills. An important factor in the success of the interviews was the interviewers' prior experience and comfort among the homeless. The team found that the purpose of the census interview needed to be clearly stated very early in the interview (so that the homeless person did not conclude that this was a public assistance interview), and the confidential nature of the information needed to be underlined.

In another ethnographic study of homelessness contracted by the Census Bureau, Glasser (1991) found that in Windham, Connecticut, the most frequent category of homelessness was the doubled-up category. Here one family (the "host" family) had agreed to take in another family (the "guest" family). Both families were most often poor, and in many cases, Latino (15 percent of Windham is Latino). Because the site of this arrangement was usually a rented apartment, there were many constraints on how long the doubled-up situation could last. Therefore, there was much instability in doubled-up households, as guest families moved either into another double-up or into a shelter, or, in some cases, found an apartment of their own (in which case, they often became a host family!).

The Census Bureau's April 1 regular household census instructions directed the head of the host household to include in their form *all* those staying with them who had nowhere else to go. There was an additional section where the respondent was asked to write in the names of persons whom they were unsure about including in their census form. Glasser's study found, though, that the host family heads did not think of the guest family as being "a part of their household" or of really being "with them." In other words, the concern about not getting into trouble themselves for giving aid to a homeless family appeared to outweigh the Census form instructions, and it seemed unlikely that doubled-up families (referred to as 'subfamilies' in Census terminology) would be counted. The doubled-up situation also tended to be the most common precursor to entering a family homeless shelter in Windham (Glasser 1991).

In the year 2000, the Census Bureau will be moving toward a service-based, daytime/evening count, that will involve an interview with individuals eating at soup kitchens and mobile food vans, or living in shelters and perhaps street encampments (Smiley 1998). There will not be an attempt to provide a count of the homeless population, but rather, an effort to include the homeless in the general enumeration. The experience of the homeless count in 1990 appears to have led to the conclusion that the middle-of-the-night hunt for the sleeping quarters of the homeless in the United States is essentially futile, and that homeless people need to be interviewed in places which they have chosen to frequent.

In contrast to the United States experience, homeless (houseless) enumerators in India during the 1991 decennial census had a full three weeks to learn about the areas where people were sleeping on the street before interviewing them on the night of the census (Glasser 1994:116). The enumerators were urged to request more help if they felt the numbers were too great for them, and they were further instructed to include any encampments at the edge of the city (Roa 1992). Perhaps India's more organized and realistic protocol reflects a greater acceptance of the *fact* of homelessness.

There was no attempt made in the 1991 Canadian census to count the homeless. However, the federal housing agency, the Canada Mortgage and Housing Corporation, has recently sponsored studies to develop reliable methods with which to count the homeless population in Canada (Peressini, McDonald, and Hulchanski 1996), and to develop and test a homelessness data collection and management system (Aubry, Currie, and Pinsent 1996). Drawing on consultations with a panel of experts from Canada and the United States, the study concluded that a *service-based approach* to counting the homeless (e.g., drawing counts from soup kitchens, shelters, drop-in programs, and outdoor encampments) would be the most efficient and cost-effective method of enumeration, while acknowledging the limitations of this approach because it does exclude some members of the street population.

There are indications that in Canada the number of homeless people is increasing. For example, in Toronto as of October 1995, approximately 20,000 households were on waiting lists for subsidized housing. The vacancy rate in the city was at a five-year low of 0.8 percent and 16 percent of City of Toronto residents (representing 75,555 people) had their social assistance benefits cut by 21.6 percent as a provincial budgetary cost-saving measure. The 12 November, 1995 annual count of occupied shelter and hostel beds in Metropolitan Toronto indicated that 3,627 people were being sheltered, roughly 23 percent more than the previous year's count (Patychuk, Phillips, and McKeown 1996).

Attention has recently been directed to the issues faced by urban aboriginal peoples in Canada (Bobiwash 1997). There is a widespread perception and a good deal of anecdotal evidence to suggest that aboriginal peoples contribute a disproportionate number to the urban homeless population. There are several distinctive features regarding aboriginal homelessness noted by the few studies that do exist: the racism and discrimination that aboriginal peoples face in the housing market; their cycles of rural-urban migration; the poor housing conditions on reserves; and the culturally inappropriate housing that does not address the needs of extended family households (Klos 1997; Beavis, Klos, Carter, and Couchant 1997).

Refugees are another group especially vulnerable to homelessness. It can take years for those who are non-sponsored refugees (distinguished from those privately sponsored by religious and other non-governmental organizations) to settle their claims. The City of Toronto receives at least 10,000 refuges a year, many of them suffering from histories of torture and trauma. These 10,000 represent half of the total number of refugees who make their way to Canada, and 50 percent are non-sponsored (Mayor's Homelessness Action Task Force 1998: 10-11). Many refugees endure discrimination, language difficulties, and high rental costs.

Methodological Issues

A bias that continues to plague most descriptions of homelessness is their reliance on the cross-sectional, or one-point-in-time study of the homeless, in which the more chronically homeless tend to be interviewed (Robertson, Koegel, and Ferguson 1989). There is also often no true sampling strategy and so it is difficult to generalize findings from many studies beyond those people interviewed by the researchers. Further, it is often difficult to *compare* studies. Since no complete listing of the homeless exists in any area, how can one develop a "sampling frame" to ensure that each homeless person has an equal chance of being selected for a study? A further critique of methodology is that the earliest generation of homelessness research tended to rely on interviewing the *sheltered* homeless, and the generalizations from these studies fall short when applied to those people living in locations out-of-doors. Even getting a complete list of shelters (especially small, informal shelters or church basements) can be more complicated than one would imagine.

To remedy some of these issues, Burnam and Koegel developed a sampling methodology in a study of the extent of mental illness among the homeless in Los Angeles. They focused on three possible sites for finding the homeless: shelter beds, meal programs (such as soup kitchens), and indoor congregating places such as missions and drop-in centers. First the team determined the extent to which users of each of these services *did not utilize* the other two services. They found that 49.3 percent of the shelter bed users did not use the other services, 44 percent of the meal-program users did not use the other services, and 6.7 percent of the indoor-congregating areas did not utilize the other services. In the final survey, a total of 462 indi-

viduals were sampled (with the goal of completing 300 interviews). The proportion of the sample drawn from each of the
three strata reflected the percentages of exclusive use from each
sector (beds, meals, and indoor congregating places).

The rigor of the sampling methods appears to have paid off,
and Burnam and Koegel obtained proportions of characteristics
of the homeless that seemed closer to reality than data obtained
from more opportunistic sampling strategies. For example, the
Burnam and Koegel study found 4 percent of the inner-city
homeless population to be women (in contrast to a previously
reported 18.6 percent), 27 percent to be White (in contrast to the
42 percent previously reported) and the proportion of homeless
who slept in a shelter bed versus the street was 44.2 percent to 26
percent (previously reported at 66 percent to 14 percent).

Obtaining an estimate of the exclusive use of homeless facilities was also utilized in several citywide enumeration efforts
undertaken by Louise Fournier, an epidemiologist with anthropological training, in Montreal, Quebec. Fournier (1988, 1989, and
1991) completed two census operations in Montreal by surveying
the numbers and types of mission users in a one-month period
and then in a twelve-month period. The term "mission users"
refers to all people who utilize shelters, soup kitchens, and day
centers, and perhaps reflects the dominance the churches used to
have in the provision of service to the homeless in Quebec. The
mission users were surveyed hierarchically in order to eliminate
overlap and generate an *unduplicated* count of the homeless. It
was found that in the twelve-month period there were an estimated 15,000 missions users, 8756 of whom were shelter users.
An interesting finding in this research was that some of these
shelter users were in fact formerly homeless individuals, and a
few had never been homeless! This certainly poses some intrigu-
ing questions about who is using shelters in Montreal.

Interpreting Homelessness

In addition to the issues of describing and enumerating the
homeless, there is an interesting discourse on the *creation* of

homelessness as a social problem. Mark J. Stern, a professor of social work, wrote a social history of homelessness in a now classic article (Stern 1984), at a time when the American public's attention and sympathy had become riveted on street people. He attributed a great deal of the media attention on the homeless to (1.) legal action taken in 1979 on behalf of the men of the Bowery in New York City, which resulted in a consent decree requiring New York City to provide clean and safe shelter for every homeless man and woman; (2.) a vigil held at St. Francis of Assisi Church near Madison Square Garden at the time of the 1980 Democratic Convention, which focused attention on homelessness; (3.) the publicity surrounding the photographic work of Ann Marie Rouseau *(Shopping Bag Ladies: Homeless Women Speak about Their Lives* 1981) and the ethnographic work of Ellen Baxter and Kim Hopper *(Private Lives/Public Spaces: Homeless Adults on the Streets of New York City* 1981).

Similarly well-publicized events occurred in Philadelphia and Washington, D.C., and the severe winter of 1981-82 featured grim stories of people freezing to death. Added to this were the results of the 1960s and 1970s era of deinstitutionalization, in which at least some of the people on the street appeared to be formerly hospitalized mental patients; and the recession in the winter of 1982-83, which linked homelessness to unemployment and foreclosures, raising the possibility that even "normal" people might be forced onto the street. According to Stern, all of this converged in a determination to have religious and voluntary agencies provide food and shelter. "Feeding the hungry and sheltering the homeless" became the mantra of the early 1980s. This fit in well with the first two years of the Reagan presidency, as the federal government tried to reduce its role in welfare, food stamps, federal housing, educational programs, and legal services (Stern 1984:294).

The rise of soup kitchens (see Glasser 1988) and shelters reintroduced an era of charity, not as a supplement to governmental programs, but as a primary source of help. Charity has always underlined the *differences* between giver and receiver, and serves as a powerful element of social control. In an interesting shift in who constitutes the "worthy poor," Stern hypothesizes that beginning in the 1980s, single women and children (the former "worthy poor") lost that status in the wake of the militant advocacy of the National Welfare Rights Organization, a nationwide advocacy organization for welfare recipients. Single adult men (the former "unworthy poor"), whose behavior could be docile and grateful inside soup kitchens and shelters, took their place. In further considering the tremendous response of religious and lay organizations who carried out food drives, set up shelters, and provided aid, Stern suggests:

> One of the reasons for this response was the comportment of the recipients. Although much attention was paid to their negative physical characteristics (bad smell, ulcerated sores), this was contrasted with their almost saint-like spirits. Docility and gratitude, not anger and suspicions, were the general images of the homeless. (Stern 1984:298)

There is also an interesting discussion regarding *who* in any society becomes (or should become) the main interpreter of homelessness. In a social history of the *representation* of homelessness in Albuquerque, New Mexico, during the 1980s and 1990s, anthropologist (and homeless service-provider) Michael Robertson (1991) traces the evolution of homelessness from a problem perceived to be one of transient middle-aged and elderly males (prior to the 1980s), able to be served by three small independent religious missions, to a more widespread problem of the "new homeless." This group includes families, single women with children, runaway youth, and the deinstitutionalized mentally ill, among others (Robertson 1991:144). The local problem came into real focus once the local and national media brought homelessness to people's daily consciousness. After this, came a great demand for information, and Albuquerque's service providers became the main sources of information.

There soon developed a rift between the traditional, volunteer, and often religiously motivated providers ("nonprofessionals") and the "professionals," the social workers, health workers, and administrators who worked with the homeless. An important issue now became who could provide *better* data, and it was clear that the professionals took the lead. They then became the major interpreters of homelessness in Albuquerque, and their accounts of homelessness became "a kind of gospel of the street" (Robertson 1991:141). Furthermore, because their data was more complete and better presented, their agencies became better funded.

In another analysis of the representation of the homeless and attitudes toward them, Judith Goode (1987a) reviews the social history of *gaminismo*, the phenomenon of the street child of Colombia. Here, the image of the *gamino* went from that of a romanticized, poor, dirty, but basically innocent street child (implied by the word gamin) to a much more negative and dangerous urban predator. As in the Albuquerque example, social-service providers are some of the major interpreters of the world of the street child. The social service world claimed that there were various stages of *gaminismo*, from the pre-gamin stage (children spend only a part of their time on the street, and return to their families on a regular basis), to the gamin stage (children are on the street full-time), and finally to the delinquent stage (generally former gamins over eighteen years old now fully engaged in crime). Goode hypothesizes that these categories are more inventions of the social-service world than a reflection of reality. These stages may misrepresent the actual fluidity that exists between home and street and between legitimate (though underground-economy) jobs and criminal activity.

The marriage of the epidemiological literature, which documents the broad patterns of homeless populations, with in-depth, participant observation and ethnographic approaches offers us a glimpse of the characteristics of the homeless population. As we have seen, each strategy for the study and counting of the homeless is fraught with problems, so that conclusions from studies need to be viewed cautiously. It is also interesting to consider the media and service agency representations of the homeless (images of the homeless ranging from docile and saint-like to crazy and drug-addicted) and the public's subsequent response.

Notes

1. For example, in New York City, 127 observers (decoys or plants)
   went to forty-one sites (a stratified random sample of the congregating places thought to have usually six or more homeless people
   in four census districts) and noted, on a scale of one to ten, whether
   they had been interviewed or observed by the census enumerators
   (Hopper 1992: 379). The plants reported observing enumerators at
   twenty-three of the forty-one sites. However, only thirty-eight of
   the observers were actually interviewed, and an additional eight
   were certain that they had been enumerated. A total of fifty-six
   were certain that they had *not* been counted.

Chapter 3

Explaining Homelessness

As the phenomenon of homelessness has dragged on in North America, a frequently posed question is *why* are there homeless people? In answering this question, there are, broadly speaking, two schools of thought. One school may be called the "personal pathology" school, which concentrates on *immediate* reasons why people become homeless. The focus is on problems such as alcohol or drug addiction, mental illness, and family violence, all of which make the person especially vulnerable to homelessness. The second school of thought may be called the "structural" school, which concentrates on *external* broad social conditions affecting a person's ability to maintain stable housing. These conditions include the lack of availability of affordable housing, low levels of wages and financial assistance, and patterns of discrimination based on race and ethnicity.

We believe that the most insightful homelessness research is holistic, in that it takes a broad, ecological perspective, viewing an individual's homelessness within larger processes in society. In this chapter, social and cultural conditions are discussed, and linked to the individual's experience of homelessness.

Holistic and Ecological Treatment of Homelessness

A widely used ecological model for understanding the causes of homelessness was developed by Gary Morse (1992), a psychologist whose work has influenced much of the public health research on homelessness. The Morse model offers us a perspective which takes into account a number of levels, from broadly based investigations of cultural beliefs, societal organization, and neighborhood and community networks, to the service-delivery system and the individual. Morse defines each level as follows:

cultural level (cultural attitudes towards race, ethnicity, mental illness, and addictions)

institutional level (housing and social assistance programs, criminal justice system)

community level (municipal policies and neighborhood activism)

organizational level (service eligibility, residency requirements, requirements concerning client characteristics, service-delivery problems, and service withdrawal)

individual level (characteristics of homeless people and their adaptations to homelessness)

Another ecological perspective is that developed by psychologist Paul Toro (Toro, Trickett, Well, and Salem 1991). His levels of analysis also account for the individual factors related to societal, cultural, and historical etiologies of homelessness. The main concepts of the Toro model are the following:

adaptation, including sociocultural influences, local context, and the individual's particular relationship to these

cycling of resources – searching for individual and community strengths that can be built upon, including both the indigenous resources of those who are homeless and the commitment of local people and organizations to help the homeless

interdependence principle – how alterations in conditions or aspects of social systems can affect other aspects of the system (e.g., attention to unintended consequences of policies and programs)

succession principle – historical, contextual, and temporal approaches to understanding present-day experiences of homelessness

Photo 3.1   With manufacturing gone, many U.S. cities have lost their economic base (Photo by Jason Glasser)

Both these models allow us to draw together issues of individual vulnerabilities within the broadest cultural and societal landscapes. We will explore some of the most interesting examples of these approaches.

In a social history of contemporary homelessness in the United States, Kim Hopper and Jill Hamberg (1986) explore *why* the 1980s saw such a surge of homelessness. After all, they argue, there have been periods of time in post-World War II history when there was greater poverty (the late 1950s). Hunger and malnutrition were more prevalent in the 1960s (before federal food programs such as food stamps). They point to a convergence of factors occurring in the 1970s and 1980s which resulted in homelessness. The 1970s saw bouts of economic stagnation, rising inflation, decline in real wages, the significant loss of manufacturing jobs, and high unemployment levels (Hopper and Hamberg 1986:17). There was the deindustrialization of the labor force and the move to service-industry jobs and part-time work; there was the loss of affordable housing through the tearing down of housing in the center city; the deinstitutionalization movement released the formerly hospitalized onto the streets; and there was a tightening of federal and state welfare programs. Vulnerable groups, such as psychiatric patients and poor people, found it increasingly difficult to find housing. Jennifer Wolch and Michael Dear (1993) link global economic and political forces to individual lives. Working with homeless communities in Los Angeles, they document ways in which economic restructuring (e.g. the hiring of part-time and temporary employees in both manufacturing and service sectors in order to avoid paying benefits and taxes); the erosion of affordable housing (the retreat from public housing to rent subsidies, while theoretically having the same effect of providing housing to poor people, in fact, does not); the divergent geography of jobs and housing (the mismatch between the location of low-skill employment and low-income housing); and the dismantling of the welfare state (the significant restrictions on eligibility, duration and amount of financial assistance, under the rubric of welfare "reform") all push individuals to become and remain homeless.

The condition of the shelters themselves may also be seen as part of the holistic look at homelessness. Ellen Baxter and Kim Hopper (1981) were able to show that some homeless preferred to stay on the streets of New York rather than use the only other option available to them – city shelters. The violence in the city shelters provided an ample deterrent to their use, and the decision to remain on the streets could be understood as involving a rational, albeit constrained, choice and "careful weighing of the personal costs involved" (Hopper 1988: 157). From their systematic field notes the researchers observed the following:

> Men's Shelter: I arrive at 5:00 p.m. in time to witness an argument becoming a scuffle as two younger men wrestle an older man to the ground and begin to go through his pockets. The older man's efforts at fending off his assailants are rather feeble and ineffective. The noise quickly draws three cops from the Shelter, the entrance to which is maybe twenty feet way. On their arrival, the two younger men take off and the older man, bleeding from the lip, is helped into the Shelter. One cop, in apparent disgust, yells after the retreating pair: "You should have known he'd have nothing worth taking." What little the old man did have in his

pockets lies strewn on the sidewalk: packets of sugar, some twine, a belt. The next man coming along carefully sifts through them. (Baxter and Hopper 1981: 56)

In addition to the people on the street, there are the groups of people at high risk of *becoming* homeless. Casting the homelessness net widely led researchers Kearns, Smith, and Abbott (1991) to conclude that thousands of New Zealanders were experiencing *incipient* homelessness. These are the people living with their friends and relatives temporarily, in places they cannot afford, in housing from which they are about to be evicted, or in inadequate dwellings such as cars, garages, and sheds (Kearns, Smith, and Abbott 1991:369). The literally homeless (those on the streets and in the shelters) then represent only the "tip of the iceberg" of homelessness. Before the 1980s, New Zealand had a reputation as one of the best-housed countries in the world, but, in recent decades, successive governments (including the traditionally egalitarian Labour Government) have shifted the responsibility for housing from the public to the private sector. Further, poverty and incipient homelessness tend to be concentrated in female-headed, Maori, and Pacific Island households living in Auckland, one of the country's two major cities.

An interesting approach to the study of homelessness is to determine the types of neighborhoods from which homeless people come. In studies from New York City and Philadelphia, Culhane, Lee, and Wachter (1996) mapped the prior addresses of 9,160 (Philadelphia) and 71,035 (New York City) families entering homeless shelters over a five- and seven-year period of time. In general the prior neighborhoods were associated with a high concentration of poor, African-American, female-headed households with young children. These are neighborhoods with relatively high numbers of youth, elderly, or immigrant populations. They also contain high rates of unemployment, crowding, abandoned buildings, housing vacancies, and high rent-to-income ratios in comparison with other areas of the city (Culhane, Lee, and Wachter 1996:327). The neighborhoods from which the homeless come are distinguished from other poor areas of the cities by the *extent* of the economic hardships experienced. This produces a "hollowing out" effect, in which buildings or units are likely to be left vacant. This effect is similar to one found in Hartford, Connecticut, where once vital working-class and poor neighborhoods are now lined with abandoned buildings (but for the existence of squatters and the drug trade) (Glasser 1997). At times, homeless people themselves have been able to articulate the constraints and conditions, both personal and structural, which have contributed to their being homeless:

> They say homeless folk are on drugs, are lazy and docile and uneducated. We have to change that perception. People also may say we're homeless because we've been evicted. But we have to look at the whole cycle; we have to talk about economic and social justice and about people taking their communities back. We have to talk about racism and about apartheid right here .... You have to talk about the whole thing. [Ruth Young, who was homeless for a year and half and was executive director of Parents on the Move, an organization of homeless families in New York City.] (Cited in Mathieu 1993: 173)

The Loss of "Last Resort" Housing and Gentrification

The loss of single-room-occupancy hotels (SROs), public lodging houses, and rooming houses is a cause of the severe reduction of affordable housing available to the single person. Similarly, the displacement of low-income tenants in urban neighborhoods by higher-income uses of space (e.g. condominiums, luxury apartments, office space), the process known as *gentrification*, is another cause of the loss of affordable housing.

In a social history of the single-room-occupancy hotel, Ovrebo, Minkler, and Liljestrand (1991) chronicle the rise of hotel living in the post-Civil War industrializing era; the increasing association between hotel life with the unmarried and elderly "marginalized" populations during the post-World War II era; and the current demolition and abandonment of the hotels due to social policies that have clearly favored home ownership. SROs take the form of older downtown buildings with at least twelve units and shared kitchen and bathroom facilities (Ovrebo,

Minkler, and Liljestrand 1991:78). It is estimated that between 1970 and 1980, over one million SRO units in the U.S., amounting to nearly half the total stock, were lost, with no comparable replacement housing being built (Hopper and Hamberg 1986:23).

On a cold winter night in January 1996, *New York Times* reporter John Tierney checked into a SRO. He describes the surprisingly peaceful night he spent sleeping in a $10-per-night cubicle in a Bowery lodging, grandly called the White House Hotel (the article is entitled "Save the Flophouse"). Tierney chronicles the myriad laws and regulations that have made owning and operating this kind of housing almost impossible, despite the fact that, according to the residents, the accommodations here are a lot better than sleeping outside or in a shelter. He laments the army of "reformers" who shut down similar Bowery lodging houses and the fact that no alternative housing was built. In the lobby of the hotel the next morning, he met an old man whose hands were shaking as he came off a drinking binge. Tierney comments: "If he winds up on the street, New York's crusading lawyers and other reformers will feel terribly sorry for him, but they won't rent him a warm cubicle on a winter night" (Tierney 1996:16).

The transformation of the Lower East Side from a working-class ethnic enclave to the more fashionable and much more expensive East Village in New York City is a classic example of the process of gentrification. The term is attributed to Ruth Glass (1964) who wrote about the trend in which the British gentry bought and renovated old buildings in London for their own use in the 1960s. The effects of gentrification in the United States follow earlier policies of urban renewal and highway building occurring in the 1950s that also substantially decreased the number of housing units for low-income people.

In a detailed social history of the attempted displacement of low-income tenants in the East Village (a portion of the Lower East Side) during the decades of the 1970s to the present, Christopher Mele (1995) documents the tactics, both legal and illegal, used by real estate developers to transform the neighborhood. In spite of New York City's laws against the wholesale dislodging of tenants (Mele 1995:77), redevelopment and displacement tactics changed who could afford to live in the Lower East Side (now re-marketed as the East Village). Between 1980 and 1990 the percentage of Latino residents dropped by 14.5 percent, the proportion of college-educated residents increased 14.5 percent, and the median household income increased by 19 percent (Mele 1995:75). State subsidies and incentives enabled developers to renovate buildings, and unscrupulous tactics (e.g., turning off the heat, purposely renting to drug users) convinced remaining low-income tenants to move.

Challenging the Mental Health Model

A large part of the general literature on homelessness has focused on chronic mental illness as, if not directly a cause of homelessness, then at least an important risk factor (e.g., Breakey et al. 1989; Wood et al. 1990). The significant decline of the inpatient psychiatric population in the United States, from over 500,000 in 1955 to 132,000 in 1983 (Redick and Witkin 1983) in favor of community placements (this became known as *deinstitutionalization*) occurred prior to the rise of homelessness in the United States. As some patients stopped taking their psychotropic medications, and moved from group homes and halfway houses in which they had been placed for the transition from hospital to community, more and more obviously deranged people were visible in U.S. cities.

Viewing homelessness as a psychiatric problem rather than a housing problem can be characterized as the *medicalization* of a social problem, which helps absolve the larger society of culpability. In her chronicle of government policies and media coverage of homelessness in New York City from 1984 to 1990, Arlene Mathieu (1993) demonstrates how homelessness during this period was consistently linked with mental illness. Very little attention was given to the socioeconomic contexts of diminishing low-income housing, unemployment, and ongoing cuts in government services. Mathieu shows how official policies, defined as "protecting" mentally ill people living on the street, were actually a "form of medicalization initiated by the administration to justify the removal of homeless people from public spaces" (1993: 170).

The term deinstitutionalization itself may be a misnomer, in that many of today's chronic mentally ill population in the U.S. are not old enough to have resided in former mental hospitals (Stoner 1989). They have grown up in a milieu of psychiatric patients' rights movements, regulatory protection against involuntary commitment, and new medications. Further, in an ironic twist of emphasis, Kalifon (1989) found that in a random sample of 313 psychiatric patients interviewed in Chicago, fifty-six had experienced homelessness or housing instability, and that most of these saw the hospital as a *housing resource* in their lives. They also defined access to housing as their most important problem.

Another perspective on the experience of those who are mentally ill and homeless is offered by Paul Koegel's extended fieldwork and tracking of the transitions in housing situations of a sample of fifty mentally ill people in Los Angeles. Koegel points out that the transition from homelessness to being housed, "what service providers usually define as nirvana," can in fact be "purgatory" to the individual (Koegel 1992: 10). For example, as Koegel and his team followed a group of fifty mentally ill homeless people in downtown Los Angeles for several years, they came to see that the social isolation of being re-housed was too difficult for many of the people, who eventually made their way back to the streets. This kind of insight is valuable for understanding the kinds of problems faced by homeless mentally ill adults and has clear implications in the program design of supportive housing.

The Political Economy Model and Drug Use

Widespread drug use is one of the underlying themes in the homelessness literature. One way to understand why and how the drug trade (particularly cocaine and crack) came to permeate poor neighborhoods, leaving family disintegration, neighborhood deterioration, and violence in its wake, is to look at the world economy. As an explanatory model, the political economy approach links the external political and economic process of the world to the neighborhood level. This model contrasts with an earlier understanding of drug use and distribution as a symptom of a "deviant subculture" which could be *cured* if the right treatments were found. The history of colonialism and capitalism are utilized in order to understand how neighborhoods of the formerly colonized people from Africa and the Caribbean in the United States and Canada are overwhelmed by drug trade.

A study of the underground economy – the untaxed jobs that people do in order to earn money and offer goods and services (e.g., baby sitting, fixing cars at the curbside) led Philippe Bourgois to a study of the multibillion dollar cocaine and crack trade in the late 1980s and 1990s in New York City (1995:3). Although a minority of the people with whom Bourgois lived in Spanish Harlem were using or selling drugs, those who did sell were responding to a world market of drugs that were, in the short term, lucrative. As a matter of fact, Bourgois wondered why *anyone* would want to work at minimum- or near-minimum-wage jobs, when selling crack or cocaine was an alternative. He also vividly documented the devastated neighborhoods and lives (including homelessness) that resulted from the drug trade.

In a similar fashion, Ansley Hamid (1990), through more than twelve years of field work living and working in the Caribbean communities of Brooklyn and in poor communities in Jamaica, follows the lives of a group of marijuana and crack and cocaine dealers. Hamid vividly portrays how the Rastafarians who were at the center of the marijuana trade routinely reinvested their profits into the community by owning and operating health food stores, credit unions, and clothing stores in the United States and Jamaica. In contrast, the cocaine and crack dealers, who tend to be young, spend their money on clothes and other flashy *accoutrements* of the lucrative trade, but quickly burn out. Lives are lost, children are not cared for, apartment buildings are abandoned, and people live at the very margins of society. Hamid attributes the shift from the relatively benign marijuana trade to the more lethal cocaine and crack

trade to changes in the world economy of the supply of marijuana, over which the drug dealers and users had no control.

Social Policies, Social Programs, and Homelessness

At times, social policies and programs, although apparently logical
and begun with beneficent intentions, themselves exacerbate that
which they were intended to alleviate (Carroll 1995). For example,
Andrew Maxwell (1996) brings together micro and macro perspectives in his anthropological study of squatters living in vacant
buildings in Mid-Atlantic City (a pseudonym), New Jersey. In this
example, subsidies to Mid-Atlantic City for public housing were
allocated on a per-unit basis rather than only *occupied* units in a
particular building being subsidized. It was financially rewarding
for the local housing authority to maintain approximately one
third of its public housing apartments vacant, which equaled 3,954
empty units (Maxwell 1996:73). At the same time, there were
6,500 families on the waiting list for public housing (Maxwell
1996:72). There soon developed a group of squatters who occupied
the vacant units and evolved a degree of organization and internal
structure that was perhaps surprising considering the more hap-
hazard arrangements the word "squatter" implies. In this example, the social policy of vacant units both contributed to the
housing shortage and created an alternative (squatting) that then
became the focus of the city's attention and use of resources.

At times the shelters that were established to provide
emergency housing may themselves compound a homeless
household's troubles. For example, Louisa Stark, an anthropologist living and working in Phoenix, Arizona, views shelters for
the homeless as "total institutions," defined by sociologist Erving Goffman as "a place of residence ... where a large number of
like-situated individuals cut off from the wider society for an
appreciable period of time, together lead an enclosed, formally
administered round of life" (Goffman 1961: xiii).

Alice, thirty-two years old, married and the mother of two,
living in a campground, describes to Stark her experiences of living in a shelter:

We once stayed in a shelter, and it was a nightmare. We had a tiny cubicle for the four of us. My son, who is hyperactive, was always getting into trouble. The staff – they was always shouting at him that he was getting into things he shouldn't, talking too loud, always nagging him. Of course, that just makes things worse ... And then the TV. It was always on. And the shows always seemed to be violent, which caused my son to be even more hyper ... It got to the point that we felt we were losing total control of our lives. So we moved out here by the river. It may take longer for us to find what we need [to no longer be homeless], but at least it's a more normal life for us. We tell ourselves that it's just long-term camping, like the vacations we used to take together when we had a home. It seems much more normal now. (Stark 1994: 558)

Shelters generally operate by a number of strictly enforced rules, many of which may have the cumulative effect of hindering rather than helping a person's efforts to make the transition from homeless to housed. Shelter users may have to struggle to fulfill their private roles as parents, friends, or employees while following shelter rules. From her work in New York City shelters, Ida Susser (1993) identifies ways the system may *impose* the female-headed household model on shelter users. Families may be separated from each other as children and their mothers are housed in one facility and the fathers must stay at another shelter. In addition, employment opportunities may be difficult to access if shift hours do not correspond to shelter rhythms.

Koegel also describes how shelter providers may define a homeless woman as "single," and yet from the perspective of the woman herself this label is not appropriate. "An insider's perspective ... may reveal that the woman highly values the role of wife and mother and *does*, in fact, have a partner, *does* have children who visit her in the shelter, and *does* see herself as filling those roles, even if economic factors have placed constraints on her which force her to cycle in and out of the shelter system and leave her unable to care for her children on an ongoing basis" (Lovell 1984 cited in Koegel 1988: 11). The mother without her children with her may be most interested in reuniting with them. The label "single woman" may also mask the fact that families have recently broken up and may deflate the true numbers of homeless families.

Social Practices and Cultural Values

National values may affect the development of social policies and programs designed to alleviate homelessness. In his cross-national comparison of homelessness in Great Britain, the United States, and Canada, Gerald Daly (1996) suggests that it is fruitful to compare these countries in terms of their definitions of the individual, the community, the state and civil society, the priority given to maintaining a social safety net for all citizens, and the roles that the governments play in intervening in housing creation, as well as in terms of ideas about charity (Daly 1996: 243-250). All three countries experienced a shift to a more conservative political philosophy during the 1990s, yet Britain and Canada continued to favor social policies for the "common good" in contrast with the ideal of individualism in the United States. This results in broader social support for housing that is provided by governments in the form of public housing and public subsidies. Furthermore, in the United States, private home ownership and the single-family household are generally held up as ideal models of living. Renting and communal living models are less valued, and this limits the housing options that people appreciate and are willing to consider.

The connections between homelessness and domestic violence have been increasingly recognized in the research on homeless women and their families (e.g., Novac, Brown, and Bourbonnais 1996). For women who have been abused by their partners, "home" may be a place of fear rather than a sanctuary of "domestic bliss." This research suggests that homelessness may not be quite the problem that we as a society have formulated. Instead, housing may be the problem and homelessness a solution, a suggestion put forth by Annabel Tomas and Helga Dittmar (1995) based on the results of their twelve in-depth interviews with homeless women in Great Britain. By turning to the streets, women have escaped the confines of unseeing, unhearing walls, doors, and roofs. "Under such circumstances, the concept of home as a place where one is safe is shattered. Home is a prison, a place that becomes more dangerous than anywhere else .... The fear of being found and harmed keeps many battered women on the move. It keeps many of them homeless" (Zappardino and DeBare 1992: 755 cited in Novac, Novac, and Bourbonnais 1996: 25). The implications of this kind of insight would suggest the importance of safe havens for women and children who may be fleeing abusive situations. They would then not need or be forced to brave the street. Even as women may not be safe in their homes, once on the streets they are also at great risk of violence. Ironically, many homeless women may seek safety by cultivating relationships with men – to protect them from other men.

The reasons why there are homeless people, and why their numbers are ever growing in the United States and Canada, involve a tangled complex of interrelated personal problems, housing market dynamics, social policies, labor-market structures, and deeply rooted social values. Untangling this web and elucidating how the individual man, woman, or family on the street has been affected by these complicated relationships is the challenge of any study of the homeless.

Chapter 4

Surviving the Streets

Home is your castle. It's a place where you can lay your head, you know, where you feel comfortable. It's your place, it's just a place where you can lay your head. That's what home is. Homeless, what does that mean? Homeless means you have nothing, you survive off the street, you know. You survive off your own wits. You do what you can do. If you want to talk about, food or clothing or whatever – where you sleep, where you eat, where you can get shoes ... you know, survival stuff.

(Excerpt of a 1996 interview by Rae Bridgman with a twenty-eight-year-old Métis, a crack addict who had been living on the streets of Toronto for four years.) (Bridgman 1996)

Perhaps anthropology's greatest contribution to our knowledge of homelessness has been a description and understanding of the methods of adaptation and survival in life on the streets and in the shelters. The thick, ethnographic descriptions of the daily rounds of the homeless have brought the concept of "the street" to life in these studies. As a group, anthropologists see the street (in its full metaphoric sense) as *one* of the sites for the kinds of adaptations to contemporary life that some homeless people make. The accompanying chart summarizes the range of ethnographic studies that have focused on various adaptations to homelessness.

Table 4.1 Selected Ethnographic Studies of Homeless Adaptation

Site of Study	Year	Authors	Location	Focus of Study
Skid Row	1970	James Spradley	Seattle, Wash.	urban nomads, drinking
	1974	David Levinson	Bowery, NYC	etiology of skid row
	1985	Christopher Hauch	Winnipeg, Manitoba	survival strategies
	1988	Cohen et al., Carl Cohen,	Bowery, NYC	survival strategies
	1989	Jay Sokolovsky	Bowery, NYC	survival strategies
Streets	1981	Ellen Baxter, Kim Hopper	New York City	homeless men and women
	1987	Judith Goode	Bogotá, Colombia	street children
	1991	Kim Hopper	New York City	homeless in an airport
	1992	Paul Koegel	Los Angeles	mentally ill
	1992	Jennifer Wolch, Stacy Rowe	Los Angeles	mapping mobility paths
	1996	B. Josea Kramer, Judith Barker	Los Angeles	Native Americans
Panhandling	1971	Horacio Fabrega	San Cristóbal, Mex.	begging
	1995	Brackette Williams	New York City, Tucson, Arizona	panhandling
Getting food	1988	Irene Glasser	New England city	soup kitchen
	1996	Karen Curtis	Delaware	food banks
Squatters	1995	Talmadge Wright	Chicago, Ill.	Tranquility City
	1996	Alexander Maxwell	Mid-Atlantic city	public housing
Shelters	1992	Kostas Gounis	Bronx, NYC	shelter life/men
	1994	Robert Desjarlais	Boston	mentally ill
	1993	Elliot Liebow	Washington D.C.	shelter life/women
Doubling-up	1991, 96	Janet Fitchen	Rural New York	rural poverty
	1996	Anna Lou Dehavenon	New York City	emergency assistance

Ethnographic Approaches

In order to enter the world of the homeless, it is necessary to develop various approaches to the challenging task of invading the private space of a person whose life is conducted so often in public view. In the following excerpt, Kim Hopper discusses his methods of approaching the homeless – in this case, in a metropolitan airport that had become home for several dozen people.

> As befitted an exploratory study, the interviews (with homeless men and women, airport authorities and concession workers) were largely unstructured. For the most part, I worked in the late night hours, after normal airport traffic had dispersed, or in the early morning before it began. When approaching homeless informants, I made offers of food and coffee; I spoke with some for hours at a time, with others only a few minutes, always making clear that I was simply interested in why people preferred the airport to the public shelter and how they managed to survive. In a few instances of obviously disoriented, badly deteriorated and hapless folks, I was able to engineer placements with agencies in the city ... But for the most part, I sought simply "the native's point of view" on this unusual habitat. (Hopper 1991: 156)

A very useful technique that has been employed in homelessness research is *triangulation*, which involves obtaining multiple perspectives (e.g., interviews complemented by extensive observations) about the same person. A good example from the work of Paul Koegel (1992) is the self-report of a homeless man on the street who maintained that he used no services, despite living on the street full-time (Koegel 1992:11). As a member of the research team tagged along with him one Sunday, they observed him obtaining an entire week's worth of food from a mobile feeding program, which he put in his ice chest (well-camouflaged inside a tattered box), thoroughly belying his claim of "no contact."

If a realistic portrayal of homelessness is to be achieved, it is incumbent on the researcher to capture the *dynamic* quality of life on the streets as people cycle through the various alternative places to sleep (the street, shelters, hotels, and rehabilitation programs). For example, interview someone after a long hotel stay, and they may discuss the loneliness and danger of their life. Interview the same person after a stint in a rehabilitation program (e.g., detoxification, or alcohol or drug treatment), and they may bitterly complain about the regimentation and lack of privacy. It is important to know where in the cycle we are meeting the person (Koegel 1992). Cycles of living on the streets may be seasonal, as has been observed among some groups of aboriginal people in Canadian cities; they spend several months living on the streets, interspersed with several months "up North" on a reserve (Beavis, Klos, Carter, and Couchant 1997).

There are some inherent challenges to the person engaged in an ethnographic study of the homeless. Most often the researchers are members of the (housed) middle class and are from the same country as the population studied. Unlike anthropologists in the past, who moved to and lived with the people of the culture under study, present-day homeless researchers make many transitions between participant observation on the streets and in soup kitchens and shelters, and their academic and personal lives. The inherently awkward quality of the research process is captured by the words of Baxter and Hopper (1981) as they interact with Albert, one of their homeless key informants. The following observations are taken from remarks from the field notes of their seminal study, *Private Lives/Public Spaces*:

> As I arrived at the hotel, Albert greeted me saying: "I tried to reach you at the office all day. They told me you had gone to the field." I squirmed with uneasiness at hearing him call his home "the field," but either my response or the actual work delighted him so much that ever since, his parting words inevitably make reference to leaving, looking for, having coffee, talking or wandering in "the field." (Baxter and Hopper 1981: 18)

Another important challenge in doing what is sometimes referred to as "domestic" anthropology is the fact that those whom one describes on the street (the homeless *and* the service providers) may very well read what is written about them (see Caroline Brettell's aptly titled book, *When They Read What We Write: The Politics of Ethnography*, 1996b). There is also the important problem of transcending what we *think* we know about our own society in order to enter another culture within our midst.

Skid Row Studies

James Spradley (1970), an anthropologist whose pioneering ethnographic work inspired a generation of anthropologists, studied the men on Skid Road in Seattle, Washington, a street lined with flop houses, taverns, and gambling houses. Spradley conducted his research during the late 1960s, as public drunkenness was becoming decriminalized and new emphasis was being placed on treatment for alcoholism. The research took place when homelessness was still considered to be characteristic of certain areas of a city (i.e., skid row), before its diffusion to greater areas of U.S. cities. Spradley brought his skills as a linguistic anthropologist to a study of the insider's worldview of life on Skid Row. This research on "urban nomads" (as Spradley termed the men) was undertaken at a time when anthropology was beginning its transition from a field whose expertise was to study societies and cultures in countries "far from home" to a discipline which increasingly looks at one's own society. Spradley's emphasis on careful methods of understanding the worldviews of these urban nomads tried to minimize the biases most researchers bring to studies of their own culture.

Spradley systematically asked where people on Skid Row slept and how they evaluated each sleeping place or "flop." Spradley set up a taxonomy of "flops" – e.g., paid hotel rooms, railroad cars, missions, all-night laundromats, and bus depots – which enabled men on the streets to make decisions about where to sleep for the night. There were fifteen dimensions of contrast that men used in order to evaluate their nightly flops. Ultimately, Spradley identified thirty-five types of flops which could be compared by at least eight attributes. For example, how much did the place cost? What was the protection from the elements? Could one lie down fully? What were the restrictions on drinking? Were there requirements (such as prayer) involved? (See chart.) In

Table 4.2 Dimensions of Contrast for Flop Domain

1.0 Monetary resources
   1.1 Not required
   1.2 Required to pay for the flop
   1.3 Required to pay for something else

2.0 Atmospheric conditions (weather)
   2.1 Almost no protection
   2.2 Out of the rain/snow
   2.3 Out of the wind
   2.4 Out of the wind, possibly out of the cold
   2.5 Out of the wind and rain/snow
   2.6 Out of the wind and rain/snow, possibly out of the cold
   2.7 Outofthewind, rain/snow, and cold

3.0 Body position
   3.1 May lie down
   3.2 Must sit up
   3.3 Should sit up but may lie down

4.0 Intoxication
   4.1 Must be sober
   4.2 Must be drunk
   4.3 Any state of intoxication

5.0 Drinking restrictions
   5.1 Low risk drinking
   5.2 High risk drinking
   5.3 Purchase drinks

6.0 Civilian interference
   6.1 Waitress
   6.2 Night watchman
   6.3 Bartender
   6.4 Manager
   6.5 Owner
   6.6 Farmer
   6.7 Engineer
   6.8 Tramps
   6.9 Anybody
   6.10 Minister or priest
   6.11 Truck driver
   6.12 Probably no civilian

7.0 Police interference
   7.1 Police check and may also be called
   7.2 Policecheck
   7.3 Police must be called
   7.4 Police do not interfere

8.0 Security
   8.1 Public/concealed/protected
   8.2 Public/concealed/unprotected
   8.3 Public/unconcealed/protected
   8.4 Public/unconcealed/unprotected
   8.5 Non-public/conceaed/protected
   8.6 Non-public/concealed/unprotected
   8.7 Non-public/unconcealed/unprotected

9.0 Urban location
   9.1 In town
   9.2 Out of town
   9.3 Either location

10.0 Permission
   10.1 Required
   10.2 Not required

11.0 Number of nights
   11.1 One night a month
   11.2 Three nights a month
   11.3 Every night of the year
   11.4 Ticket to hotel

12.0 Requirements: listening (earbanging), praying (nosediving)
   12.1 Neither action necessary or important
   12.2 Neither action necessary, listening important
   12.3 Neither action necessary, both important
   12.4 Listening necessary, praying important

13.0 Work opportunities
   13.1 Work at the mission
   13.2 Work out of the mission
   13.3 Work at and out of the mission

14.0 Meals
   14.1 Mealticket
   14.2 Soup and sandwiches

15.0 Clothes
   15.1 Available
   15.2 Not available

Source: James P. Spradley. *You Owe Yourself a Drunk.* (Boston: Little, Brown and Company, 1970). p. 110.

Spradley's view, men on Skid Row were forced into creating a culture of the streets because they had been rejected by family, friends (apart from other men like themselves), and employers. Their repeated incarcerations cut them off further from any stability they might have known. Mobility became a way of life. "The tramp is on a perpetual journey and the trip is more important than the destination" (Spradley 1970: 254).

In an ethnography of men on New York's Bowery (its equivalent to Skid Row), David Levinson (1974) found life for the homeless to be rapidly changing as the population became younger and more violent. One old-timer reflected: "Fifteen years ago I could sit down here (on the sidewalk), lean back, and go to sleep with fifty dollars in my pocket and no one would bother me. Now I get hit over the head for a dime. It's no good, too rough" (Levinson 1974: 26).

Levinson identified separate groups of men on the Bowery. These were the workers (steady drinkers who worked on the Bowery, or away from it, but came back when not working); elderly pensioners who received checks; full-time alcoholics; and (increasingly) drug addicts, who tended to be young African-American men whose allegiances appeared to be in neighborhoods away from the Bowery. (They were placed there by city agencies in order to have an address from which to receive welfare.) In this ethnography, which included a period of time when Levinson himself posed as an unemployed ex-G.I., he documented the tendency of the older alcoholics to fear the young drug addicts because at times they broke into sleeping cubicles and stole money from them. The addicts' view of the alcoholic men was also one of disdain.

More than ten years after the Levinson study, Cohen and his colleagues (1988) (see also Cohen and Sokolovsky 1989) again turned their attention to the survival strategies of older men on the Bowery. Their study was characterized by more statistical rigor than earlier skid row studies: approximately 10 percent of the estimated 2700 men over age fifty living in flophouses, apartments, and on the surrounding streets of the Bowery were sampled during the study period of 1982-83. The methodology of the study involved participant observation,

intensive interviewing, and semi-structured questionnaires utilizing previously tested measures of physical, mental, and
socioeconomic well being, as well as measuring the degree of
social interaction of older people.
This study showed that the men were chronically short of
cash, and, that life on the Bowery offered very inexpensive survival. Only 16 percent of the men had incomes above the poverty
level ($5,061 for a single person in 1983). Most of the men, the
authors believed, were entitled to more financial assistance than
they were receiving. In order to get some cash, many of the men
worked for the flophouses or panhandled. They also pooled their
money and borrowed from each other. Hot meals were obtained
from soup kitchens and missions in the Bowery. A favorite place
for the men in the study was the Bowery Residents' Committee,
which had a publicly funded seniors' lunch. This program
excluded younger men, whom the older men feared.

In order to find a secure place to sleep, men either paid for
a cubicle in a hotel (when they had money) or slept in small
groups in the park. However, it was hard to relax: "I can stretch
out but I can't relax my body, lay down and sleep. It's no joke sitting up in a hard bench sleepin'. Everytime somebody passes I'm
woke. My nerves is on edge 'cause I've seen people attacked in
the park" (Cohen, Teresi, Holmes, and Roth 1988: 62).

Some of the men slept outside in the summer and paid for
a cubicle in the winter months. The typical lodging house on the
Bowery was described by the authors:

> Entering the typical lodging house the visitor encounters a rather
> steep, dusty, dimly lit imitation marble staircase with wooden
> banisters on either side. The men are housed in 4' by 7' cubicles
> with a bed, a locker, a night table, and whatever personal posses-
> sions the occupant can squeeze into his space. Each cubicle is sep-
> arated from the adjoining one by a thick wall that extends only
> part way to the ceiling, the resultant space filled with a 2 foot
> wide strip of chicken wire. In the ticket hotel (hotels used by the
> Men's Shelter) there are usually several large dormitories on var-
> ious floors. The dormitories are dimly lit, smelly, dirty, crowded
> hovels consisting of sheets and not uncommonly infested with
> lice or chiggers. The cheapest flops charge about $87 per month
> whereas the better ones charge about twice as much. (Cohen
> Teresi, Holmes, and Roth 1988: 62)

Most of the men appeared to be resigned to their lot. For example, although 64 percent reported mice or roaches in their dwellings, only 20 percent considered this a problem (Cohen Teresi, Holmes, and Roth 1988: 62). The real dangers of the street were getting mugged and constantly owing money to the loan sharks, some of whom got all of the men's monthly checks.

The area of greatest need was health care. The health care the men obtained from the hospitals and public clinics was seen as inconsistent and lacking in follow-up. The authors strongly recommended that the social-service agencies of the Bowery, upon which the men were relying more and more, add health services to their repertoire of help.

Cohen and his colleagues were most impressed by the intense reciprocal sharing of resources among the men on the Bowery. The social and material support the men got from each other served as a buffer to the harsh life on the streets and in the flophouses. Such reciprocity and sharing is also highlighted in Christopher Hauch's study of "binge spending" on skid row in Winnipeg, Manitoba. He suggests that the capacity of skid-row residents to save money is inevitably eroded by the threat of robbery. Generosity and redistribution of new-found wealth, according to Hauch, represents an adaptive response to disperse swiftly what could become a liability and place one in great physical danger (Hauch 1985:44-48).

Life on the Streets

Contemporary studies of the life on the streets of homeless people can be said to have begun with the work of Ellen Baxter and Kim Hopper (1981) in New York City. This team, a psychologist and an anthropologist, interviewed and observed homeless adults on the streets. In judging who was homeless, and therefore a person to be approached, they were guided by the following definition: "... those whose primary nighttime residence is either in the publicly or privately operated shelters or in the streets, in doorways, train stations and bus terminals, public plazas and parks, subways, abandoned buildings, loading docks

Photo 4.1 Stash of sleeping bags and blankets (Toronto) (Photo by Rae Bridgman)

and other well-hidden sites known only to their users" (Baxter and Hopper 1981: 6-7). The two driving questions of their research were: why has the person become homeless in the first place? And what is the nature of the public help (shelter and food) available for the homeless person?

Although many of the people on the street interviewed in this study appeared to have mental health problems (e.g., talking loudly to themselves, telling the interviewers about imaginary people), Baxter and Hopper point out that the daily stresses of life on the street can themselves be mentally exhausting and disorienting. For example:

> Private shelter: A Chinese woman in her early seventies, with no family or friends nearby, had lived alone in an apartment until a gang of youths began stalking her at the beginning of each month for her social security check. Eventually they took everything she owned – her identification cards, address book of distant friends, purse and valuables. She was found by the police wandering the street and taken to a shelter. She speaks in a whisper or writes messages on scraps of paper for fear of being overheard by "bad people" like those who destroyed her life. (Baxter and Hopper 1981: 43)

Rather than seeing mental illness as a *cause* of homelessness, Baxter and Hopper see symptoms as the *effect* of life on the streets and in shelters. In fact, the symptoms of mental illness expressed by many homeless (e.g., pacing, rummaging through the garbage, talking to oneself) can be difficult to distinguish from behaviors that may arise as survival adaptations to homelessness – what Hopper refers to as the "more florid street symptomatology" (1988: 158). Furthermore, acting "crazy" may be an effective strategy for keeping other people at a distance.

Baxter and Hopper presented the survival patterns of people on the street as rational responses to their condition. The researchers asked how homeless people met their needs for shelter, food, and security, in light of their personal resources (e.g., income, ability to read and write, general appearance) and the opportunities offered within their total environment (e.g., employment, lodging, friends, and family). The authors also tried to communicate the great *flux* in adaptive strategies, and warned against seeing each element in those strategies as discrete and static.

According to Baxter and Hopper, if a person would not or could not live in a shelter, he or she often found an abandoned building, a spot on the street over a heating grate, or a subway tunnel under the city streets in which to sleep. Some rode the subway all night, and some kept walking and tried to sleep in the daytime. One photographic study of people living on the streets of New York City (Balmori and Morton 1993) has documented poignant attempts to make living out-of-doors aesthetic, with gardens and modest landscaping created by the homeless (see photo, "Jimmy's Garden").

In his research on the use of the contemporary landscape as shelter, previously referred to in chapter four, Kim Hopper (1991) studied a group of homeless people who lived, for various periods of time (from several days to several years) in an airport in New York City. Earlier studies of airport residents had presented them as mentally ill individuals who were attracted to the airport as a symbol of flight and wandering (e.g. Weller and Jauhar 1987). Hopper, on the other hand, found a group of homeless people who utilized the airport on a transient, permanent, or seasonal (winter) basis because, as a *survival niche* (Hopper's term), the

Photo 4.2 Jimmy's Garden (Photo by Margaret Morton)

airport offered clean bathrooms, snack bars and cafeterias for purchasing or scavenging meals (supplemented by an informal system of charity provided by the food-service workers), and excellent sleeping accommodations. Added to this was the benign attitude of the airport workers and the ability of at least some of the homeless to pass as stranded travelers, who often use their bags and the floor for a bed (Hopper 1991: 163-164).

Jennifer Wolch, a geographer, and Stacy Rowe, an anthropologist, documented the mobility (in the form of time-space maps) and social networking of homeless men and women within the Los Angeles area (Wolch and Rowe 1992). Their work, through eighteen months of participant observation and forty-two in-depth interviews, enabled them to chart, in great detail, the mobility paths of the homeless as they made their way in search of food, income, social support, and rudimentary shelter (see map). These maps can then be used as a guide indicating where to position services for the homeless. Two types of mobility pathways were noted. The first was the individual's daily path or routine of travel in order to meet basic needs. The second was the individual's life path – movement into and out of homelessness. This research indicates that when the person was not successful in meeting daily needs for food, shelter, and camaraderie, long-term goals were often sacrificed.

In their daily quest to meet their survival needs, the men and women in this study had two types of social networks. The *homed* network was formed by family, friends, and social-service providers. The *homeless* network consisted of the people they saw as they made their daily rounds – their panhandling clients, the business people they saw, and the other homeless people. The homeless network itself was often a buffer from the dangers of the street. People watched each other's belongings, told each other about day jobs, shared food and information, and generally defended each other. For example, a woman Wolch and Rowe call Sharon Adams (also known as "Mom," a common appellation among groups where fictive kinship is important) says:

> I felt secure. Because of the people that I'm with in my camp ... I haven't had any really scary situations where somebody's tried to mug me or anything like that ... Everywhere I go, somebody's

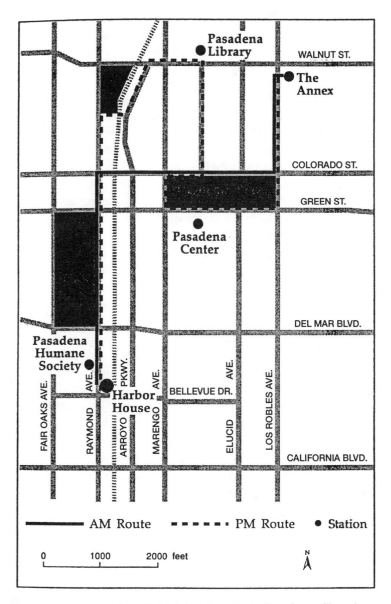

Figure 4.1 Frank Rossi's Mobility Routine in Pasadena (Chart by Jennifer Wolch and Stacy Rowe)

hollering, "Hi Mom! Hi Mom!" I told the police that one time this one guy came in the camp [trying to] fool with me, "he won't make it off this beach, Officer, too many people will kick his ass, and if you don't believe me, look at all those people coming off the sand and around the bike path and from down that way." (Wolch and Rowe 1992: 127)

These social ties greatly affected the people's self-esteem, and, according to Wolch and Rowe, ultimately helped people take steps to leave the streets. The researchers viewed some types of services as more inviting than others for the striking up of friendships and the formation of mutual support networks. For example, the laissez-faire, low-demand day shelter, St. Mary's, provided food, day shelter, laundry facilities, showers, and bathrooms. There was a minimum of staff pressure, and social networks flourished. On the other hand, Harbor House, the substance-abuse rehabilitation center that also provided day services, was more demanding of the homeless clients (their goal was to get people into their recovery programs). Wolch and Rowe saw this "higher demand" shelter as less instrumental in the development of friendships.

As positive as the relationships on the street appeared in the Wolch and Rowe study, some were based on activities that would not help the person leave the state of homelessness. Examples were the camaraderie formed by mutual drug and alcohol use, or the physical and emotional abuse suffered in some relationships.

There was ambivalence expressed by some of the people in this study about totally leaving homeless friends behind once permanent housing was obtained. This reluctance to leave the streets has been noted by others. For example, Todd G. Pierce (1992) termed this phenomenon "going back for the others," a metaphor from the military. Pierce found that in fact many of the homeless on the streets of Hartford, Connecticut, were veterans of the Vietnam War and were very reluctant to leave others behind once their own situation had improved. This search for camaraderie has been recognized by some programs which provide transitional and permanent housing for the homeless, as they incorporate close social interaction into their housing programs.

In another study of the mobility patterns of homeless people in and around the skid row area of Los Angeles, Wolch, Rahimian, and Koegel (1993) found that the people who experienced the most daily mobility in and around Los Angeles were not "drifters" or "nomads" but people trying to meet their daily needs for food, shelter, income and employment, health care and human services, and social interaction/support. Those newest to homelessness, or those who were in and out of homelessness, were most likely to maintain links to family and friends outside of skid row (and obtain resources from them), and thus were the most mobile. One of the practical suggestions from this study was that although this mobility was adaptive, the costs involved in transportation were enormous. The provision of low-cost bus passes to homeless people could facilitate their functional and adaptive daily mobility paths. It was the longer-term – chronically homeless who were not leaving skid row. They were relying on the missions and agencies in that area for all of their needs.

Finally, some of the mobility observed in this study was seen to be an unnecessary drain on resources. The constantly changing welfare regulations and the fragmentation of services meant that homeless people were spending much of the day pursuing their checks. Difficulty in obtaining welfare has often been seen as part of an effort to deter people from applying (see Piven and Cloward's classic *Regulating the Poor*, 1971). Also, the reason that many of the people moved into skid row in the first place was due to the lack of services in their home communities. The phenomenon of having the cities be the repositories of services for the poor has made many people in U.S. cities bitter, as they are expected to absorb the costs (social and financial) of people from outlying regions that refuse to aid their own residents (Glasser 1996).

In a study of homeless older American Indians living in Los Angeles, Kramer and Barker (1996) noted an adaptive pattern of mutual assistance in life on the streets. The research was carried out utilizing interviewers who were themselves older American Indian adults, and who, in addition to acting as interviewers, became *de facto* case managers for homeless native elders with health and social-service needs. It was found that younger men lived in an area called "Apache Alley" and formed a protective ring around women, the disabled, and the elderly. One elderly woman living in a SRO was recognized as the mother figure for the homeless community; newcomers sought her out for information and assistance (Kramer and Barker 1996: 400).

In all three of the Los Angeles homeless studies just discussed, it is important to recall that living outside in southern California, with its benign climate, does not pose the dangers of living outside in more northern climes, although fatalities from hypothermia and burns from fires in encampments are not uncommon.

Positive social networks and fictive kin relationships among the homeless have been themes running through much of the literature on street children in developing countries, such as the work of Einar Hanssen in Sri Lanka (1996) and Judith Goode in Colombia (1987a). In Colombia, the street children (*los gaminos*) form *galladas*, which are hierarchical gangs with specific rules of behavior, division of labor, and territoriality (identification with certain streets for the purposes of working). During the day, children move around in small groups within these designated territories, working in the informal economy (shining shoes, selling food, panhandling, cleaning car windshields). At night they come back to the larger group and pool their resources. The system of redistribution of income is the *promis*, in which the income goes to the *gallada* to be used for common domestic life (food, shelter, and recreation). *Camadas* are the hidden sleeping places of the group.

Goode presents the above as existing in the "golden age" of *gaminismo*, in the 1960s and 1970s, when street children were perceived primarily as innocent and nonviolent victims of poverty and political disruption in Colombia. Now street children are feared, and there is a sharp rise in violence and male and female prostitution among the *gaminos*. Goode cites reports of women in Bogotá having earrings ripped from their ears by the *gaminos* and their fingers cut off in order to remove rings (Goode 1987a: 7). Further, the social organization of the *galladas* has broken down, so that now these groups have very fluid boundaries and lack the mutual protection of the past. The range of conditions of street children presented by Goode is corroborated by three fictionalized portrayals of children on the street. The films *My Home, My Sky (1990), Salaam Bombay* (1986), and *Pixote* (1981) present varying views of the mutual support street children give each other, from benign to violent (see Glasser 1995 for reviews of the films).

Panhandling

A common method of survival on the street is panhandling, or begging for money. There are few anthropological studies on begging, which is perhaps surprising given the attention of anthropologists to life on the streets. An early and excellent study of begging was conducted by Horacio Fabrega (1971), a psychiatrist and anthropologist. The study took place in San Cristóbal de las Casas, in Chiapas, Mexico, a city famous its many churches and for the number of beggars (*limosneros*) asking for alms, (*limosnas*). The region is very poor and was more recently the site of the Zapatista uprising, in which rebels demanded that the indigenous people of Mexico share in the wealth of the nation.

Fabrega studied the phenomenon of begging in San Cristóbal by means of participant observation, interviews, gathering life histories, and, in some cases, performing medical evaluations on over eighty beggars. He sought to include beggars from a variety of locales, including the churches, the market, and the plaza. The beggars were approximately 50 percent Latino (i.e., Spanish-speaking, wearing western-style clothing, and identifying with the national culture) and 50 percent Indian (Mayan). Most were male, and many came from the surrounding countryside. The majority of the beggars were physically sick or old, and had no kin who could help them. They had few formal sources of help, and begging offered the social contact with other people that was essential to their survival.

There appeared to be a relationship between a person's physical disability and his characteristic manner of asking for alms. The people with obvious physical disabilities needed only to sit or stand next to the doorway of a church, with hand extended or a plate next to them. Those without an obvious disability had to do more to convince a potential donor of their need for charity. The residents of San Cristóbal felt it was their religious obligation to give alms. Further, most of the beggars in this study were able to "borrow" a place to sleep for the night on the patio of someone's house. They generally would leave in the early morning, and were not permitted inside the house.

Despite the beneficence of some residents of San Cristóbal towards the beggars, most of those interviewed by Fabrega expressed shame at having resorted to begging for survival. They hoped that no one from their home communities would see them. The residents of San Cristóbal saw the beggars as socially inferior and unclean, and spoke to them in the *tu* form (informal) regardless of the beggars' ages.

Twenty-five years after the San Cristóbal study, Brackette Williams (1995) sought to observe begging in two U.S. cities, New York and Tucson, Arizona. Her mission was not to conduct a systematic study, but rather to become a more informed "fellow citizen" in a society where panhandling is no longer confined to skid row. After several years of observation, Williams described three types of beggars: the "character beggars" who impressed listeners with their stories and personalities; the "brother-can-you-spare-a-dime" beggars, whose interactions with fellow urbanites were brief and whose stories were minimal; and the "will-work-for-food beggars." There were an ample number of character beggars on Williams' daily subway ride in New York City:

> As the train pulls out of the 14th Street station, a man enters the train from a rear adjoining car ... His feet are bare and crusted with dirt and sores, some healed, the other not ... From his breastbone to the top of his pants cascades a ragged incision with black stitches and staple-like metal clamps .... He begins his spiel:
>
> "Good morning, ladies and gentlemen. I am sorry to disturb you. I have just been released from the hospital. I have applied for public assistance, but it will be some time before the money starts to come. I am homeless; I cannot work. I am forced to beg to keep alive until the money from public assistance comes. I appreciate any help you give me. Thank you. God bless you." (Williams 1995: 26)

As in Fabrega's observations, beggars underlined their lack of any alternatives, had an obvious disability (though not necessarily a permanent one), and invoked God in their expression of gratitude. As a part of her observations, Williams observed the rest of her subway riders, whose reactions ranged from a sympathetic "there but for the grace of God go I" attitude to trying to ignore the beggar. In Tucson, Arizona, where there were no subway cars, beggars stood at the intersections of highways. Their begging took the form of the "brother-can-you-spare-a-dime" brief encounter. For example:

> June 10, 1991: A white woman, middle-aged in appearance, stands on the traffic island, at the intersections of Oracle and Orange Grove Roads, in the well-to-do northwest district, just outside the city limits. She is accompanied by two rather bedraggled-looking, dirty children. As if posing for a portrait, she stands with her children beside her, the sign that labels her midsection reading "Husband Recently deceased, I must feed my children, please help. God Bless." (Williams 1995: 36)

By the late 1980s in New York City, some of the beggars had taken on a new identity: that of *vendors* of a slim newspaper, *Street News*. These vendors kept $0.75 from the $1.00 sale of the newspaper. Begging was reconstructed as selling a worthwhile item. "Good afternoon, ladies and gentlemen. I deeply regret the need to disturb you. Let me say that I am not a beggar. I am not a panhandler. I am a homeless vendor, selling *Street News* to help myself. Currently I am still having to live in a shelter, but I hope to save my money and I hope, soon, to be able to get an apartment for myself and my family" (Williams 1995: 33).

Williams noted that as *Street News* gained acceptance in the general public, the articles went from being directed to the homeless (e.g., a recipe for pigeon stew) to articles of more general interest (e.g., tips for the job search). In research on homelessness in Canada, Glasser, Fournier, and Costopoulos (1999) discuss a similar paper, *L'itinéraire*, which is sold on the streets of Montreal, Quebec, by *camelots* (street peddlers). At least for some of the panhandlers, working, as in the case of selling *Street News* or *L'itinéraire*, offers a supplement to or substitution for begging.

Getting Food

By the 1980s, soup kitchens and food banks, once called "emergency" feeding programs, had dropped the word emergency
from their titles and become a part of the contemporary landscape in the United States and Canada. Soup kitchens, serving
a hot noontime meal or evening dinner, and sometimes serving
breakfast as well, have come to be relied upon by people who live
on the streets and in shelters (shelters typically do not serve
meals during the day). Soup kitchens and food banks have
become so institutionalized that government officials depend on
them to supplement meager cash assistance, people in need of
doing community service and charity work depend upon their
existence to fulfill their commitments, and poor people (most of
whom are *not* homeless) depend on them for a hot meal and food
supplies. Despite their pervasiveness, soup kitchens and food
banks have not often themselves been the focus of study as
adaptations to homelessness.

One full-length treatment of soup kitchens is *More Than
Bread: Ethnography of a Soup Kitchen* (Glasser 1988). Glasser
describes a soup kitchen which served a daily hot meal to over
one hundred "guests" (as soup kitchen clients are typically
called) each day in a "no-questions-asked" setting. With very
few staff members and many hours of operation during which
guests could drink coffee, smoke cigarettes, and socialize, this
was a setting in which poor people created their own set of rules
and ambiance. While most of the guests had shelter (many in a
single-room-occupancy hotel with meager cooking facilities),
some of the living-out-of-doors homeless did come in for their
daily meal. In addition to providing food, warmth, use of a telephone, and bathrooms, the staff were able to refer guests to
other agencies and were seen as their advocates. Further, guests
themselves formed many supportive social networks and came
to each other's aid in times of crisis.

Working in food banks and soup kitchens in Delaware ten
years later, Karen Curtis (1996) found a cadre of volunteers
whose attitudes toward the recipients of the food were negative
and suspicious. Rather than the "there but the grace of God go

I" attitude exhibited by the staff and volunteers in Glasser's ethnography, Curtis observed time and energy being spent making sure that people were not receiving food they did not need. She noted physical barriers between the volunteers and guests (e.g., a small serving window where the food was handed out to each soup kitchen guest). At one (open) food bank she found people standing in the rain waiting for the food (Curtis 1996: 16). Curtis also noted that some food policies and programs directed at the poor originated not because of the nutritional needs of the poor, but out of a quest to find non-market outlets for surplus agricultural products, in order to sustain farm prices and incomes (Curtis 1996: 10). Therefore, if one wants to understand how the homeless meet their needs for sustenance by studying the feeding programs of shelters, soup kitchens, and food banks, it is useful to look not only at what is happening in the dining room, from the recipients' point of view (as in the Glasser study), but also, as Curtis points out, at the total context of the feeding program and how it is delivered.

Squatting

In the developing world, millions of people live in squatter settlements, which are self-made housing units, often at the edge of a city, inhabited by poor people who have 'invaded' the land, often at night, and built structures (Glasser 1994; Drakakis-Smith 1987). From the *pueblos jóvenes* (young towns) of Lima, Peru, to the *bidonvilles* (tin cities) of Africa, these examples of self-help are seen as incipient communities that could, with the assistance of clean water, security of tenure, and some basic services, become stable communities of productive citizens (see *Housing by the People: Towards Autonomy in Building Environments* by John Turner, 1976, for a full discussion of the potential of squatter settlements). In the industrialized world, squatting usually refers to taking over a vacant building, as we have seen in the case of public housing in New Jersey, as documented by Andrew Maxwell in chapter three, or in setting up encampments on unoccupied (but not necessarily ownerless) land.

Tranquility City, located in a deteriorated industrial district on the Near West Side of Chicago, was an encampment of twenty-two plywood huts provided by the Mad Housers (a group of architecture students) of Atlanta, Georgia, that existed from November 1991 to June 1992. The huts were insulated; each had a sleeping loft and a stove for heat and cooking. In an extensive study of the dynamics of this squatter settlement, Talmadge Wright (1995) demonstrates how men who had been used to the rules and danger of the city's shelters, or the isolation of the streets, came together in the encampment to form a mutually supportive community. According to one resident: "Tranquility City was a beautiful place .... It's peaceful, not a care in the world, nobody's bothering you, we listen to the radio, we listen to our gospel station, and you just kick back. And somebody walk up, and you ask them "you want a cold drink?" ... I seen this done in the country when people would be walking down the road, for long walks to get somewhere" (Wright 1995: 65).

Although, according to Wright, the huts provided the men with community, autonomy, and privacy, the city of Chicago saw things differently. The huts (termed "guerilla architecture" by the Mad Housers) did not have indoor plumbing and were not built according to the city's building code. Before tearing down the huts, the city offered all of the hut residents apartments in public housing. The inhabitants of Tranquility City, however, saw the huts as a resource for other homeless people who did not have access to housing. A protest galvanized around the issue of whether the huts were to stay. Ultimately the huts were carted away, but members of Tranquility City experienced a time when collective action had produced some changes, at least in their own lives. Amy Phillips, herself a Mad Houser from 1987 to 1992, and Susan Hamilton (1996) also describe the activities of the Mad Housers and homeless people. These authors document the ingenuity of both dwellers and volunteers in their use of low technology and their very effective use of media coverage to draw attention to homelessness.

Dee Southard, herself once homeless, has conducted extended research among homeless families camping on public lands in the Pacific Northwest (Southard 1992, 1994, 1996). A large part of the land in both Oregon (55 percent, 34 million acres) and Washington (45 percent, 19 million) is publicly owned (Southard 1994). Her studies of non-recreational camping bring to life some of the survival and coping strategies that "campers" adopt in their bid to maintain self-sufficiency and avoid being hassled by the authorities. One camper she interviewed explained: "I can't even imagine why anyone that's sane and sober would live in a shelter. It's only a thirty minutes drive from this campsite to town, but out here I can have some real privacy. Sometimes I only see one or two people all day long. It's not like bein' poor in a city" (Southard 1994).

Southard identifies the campers as belonging to three main groups: the "voluntarily nomadic" (for whom traveling and camping is a lifestyle preference); the "economic refugees" (who lack the resources to maintain a conventional "homed" lifestyle); and the "separatists" (moderately stationary campers who live in remote and secluded rural areas of public-owned lands) (Southard 1996).

Shelter Life

Whereas the majority of the research on homelessness in North America began in homeless shelters (see for example Burt 1992, and Fournier and Mercier 1996), many anthropologists have not focused their work on shelters, but have turned their attention more often to life on the streets. We think that there are several reasons for this. One is that anthropologists wanted to avoid the fallacy of generalizing about the state of homelessness by only making contact with people in shelters: the generalization would then be about the *sheltered* homeless, who may as a group be different (for example, more passive) than people living out-of-doors. Shelters are only one of the many possible resources offered by the urban landscape. One can sleep in a shelter, in an abandoned building, on a park bench (depending on the weather), with family or friends, or, when funds are available, even in a rented room. The state of flux experienced by many of the homeless was illustrated in Glasser's research as a shelter resident one evening explained his living situations: "… Bert [a frequent shelter resident] told me that he also lives at the YMCA, where you can have a room with no bath for $125 a week and a room with a bath for $150. When I remarked that for that amount ($500 to $600 per month), one can rent an apartment, he agreed, but said that the advantage of the YMCA (where you pay by the week) is that you have the freedom to come and go" (Glasser 1996a: 21).

Photo 4.3 Entrance to a shelter for men in Hartford, Connecticut (Photo by Jason Glasser)

Life outside is perhaps closer to the classic anthropological studies of small-scale, agricultural or pastoral societies than is life in a shelter. In studying the homeless out-of-doors, one can document the culture that is created by people living outside the conventional forms of shelter, as opposed to studying groups of people who are conforming to shelter life, a creation not of the homeless themselves, but of the religious, voluntary, or governmental body administering the shelter. Further, as a group, anthropologists, notoriously an independent lot, perhaps identify with the out-of-doors homeless.

When anthropologists have focused their attention on shelter living, they have, for the most part, been struck by the corrosive effects of shelter life on the homeless person. Robert Desjarlais (1994) spent time in a fifty-two-bed shelter for the homeless mentally ill. Although the staff regarded the shelter as the "Rolls Royce" of shelters, the place was in fact noisy and distracting. He writes of one resident:

> Alice is a fortyish native of New England who lives in a shelter of cots and partitions set up on a basketball court in the basement of a large government center in downtown Boston. If she is not staying in the shelter, she is sleeping in a psychiatric hospital or on the city's streets. She considers herself "estranged from society" since the state took her children away ten years ago; she now spends much of her time bumming cigarettes and reading the Bible ... "If I can just read the Bible for 15, 16 hours a day," she says, "and just block out all the rest, then I'm okay." Given the lack of calm in the shelter, and Alice's own troubles, the task is not an easy one. When we cross paths in the building and I ask how she is doing, she often says she is "struggling along." (Desjarlais 1994: 886)

This *struggling along*, or just existing, can be seen as a shelter-induced adaptation, and may not be primarily due to the mental illness suffered by most of the residents. According to Desjarlais, struggling along contrasts to *experiencing* life, which implies active engagement with the world, including the ability to perceive, reflect, and act. "A good day for someone who *experiences* [our emphasis] might be one in which there is a novel integration of personal undertakings, a tale to be told about events bordering on the adventuresome. The features of such a day build on the stuff of novelty, transformation, employment, and movement. A good day for someone who struggles along, in contrast, might be a smooth one, where nothing much happens, where a few bucks are earned, where the voices are not too bad, where pressure is relieved through pacing, and where there are enough cigarettes to last the day" (Desjarlais 1994: 897).

The main tool of social control in this shelter was ejection from the shelter, for varying lengths of time, depending on the infraction. The staff also frequently reminded the residents that

Photo 4.4   Inside a shelter for men in Hartford, Connecticut (Photo by Jason Glasser)

"this is not a home" and they should not become too comfortable. As a matter of fact, according to Desjarlais, the shelter director was interested in the results of his study because he wanted to make the shelter *less* accommodating to the residents (Desjarlais 1994: 899)!

Residents of the shelter spent much of the day pacing, bumming and smoking cigarettes, and drinking coffee. The description is reminiscent of Harry Murray's (1984) contrast between linear time, where people make long-term plans, and cyclical time, associated with survival goals. Life on the streets is often associated with immediate, daily, weekly, and monthly cycles of time: the hours of opening and closing of the soup kitchens and shelters, the weekly appointments with social workers and doctors, and monthly check days.

In a study of a large (600 beds) New York City shelter (Franklin Avenue shelter in the South Bronx), Kostas Gounis (1992) hypothesized that the institutionalized atmosphere of the shelter eventually resulted in the *shelterization* or dependency of the occupants. For example, rules governing time and space kept the men on the move (to leave during the day, to be in by early afternoon) or kept them waiting in line (e.g., the ubiquitous lines for food, the shower, seeing the caseworker). The men were not allowed to sleep in a bed or on the floor during the day and so resorted to sleeping on top of pool tables and ping-pong tables (Gounis 1992: 140), a sight reminiscent of the large mental hospitals before the era of deinstitutionalization. Instead of making choices for themselves, as one needs to do in order to live independently, the shelter acts as a total institution and makes decisions for its residents.

A difference between the classic total institution (the prison or mental hospital) and the shelter according to Gounis, was the *lack* of social distance between the custodial staff and the men, due to the generally undervalued position of working in a shelter. Custodial staff were often recruited from the ranks of the formerly homeless, and often engaged in an underground economy (of drugs, for example) with the residents (Gounis 1992: 132). Unlike the residents of other shelters, whose location is miles from the residents' communities, many of the men of the Franklin Men's Shelter were from the South Bronx, the same neighborhood as the shelter itself. As men were forced to move from their original households, the shelters became "community bedrooms" for people whose lack of income, crime, drug and alcohol abuse, mental illness, or physical disabilities made them no longer welcome at home (Gounis 1992: 135).

Sometimes shelters are not the stultifying warehouses we've described. For example, at one shelter Baxter and Hopper (1981) found the sheets clean and most of the men in good spirits as they watched TV before turning in to their single rooms (cubicles). "As the men prepare for bed, it is clear that many on this floor are regulars. The tiny rooms are filled with possessions (radios and mementos), their walls lined with pictures ... A friendly, bunkhouse repartee peppers the air, as men retire" (Baxter and Hopper 1981: 52).

This sense of community and social interaction becomes important in designing programs for the formerly homeless (see chapter five). For example, in her research on StreetCity in

Toronto, Rae Anderson found that some residents of this housing designed for the homeless said that they did not want the isolation of ordinary apartment living (Anderson 1997: 9). A "Main Street" corridor in the middle of the converted warehouse, StreetCity, offers the camaraderie so often noted in ethnographies of street life. "The Main Street partakes of a conception of urban space that is partly theatrical. The daily flurry of common activities, and the dynamic comings and going on Main Street offer a carnival of social interaction that carries with it a unifying potential" (Anderson 1997: 10).

Observers of shelter life have noticed the great variability among shelters. Elliot Liebow (1993), in a richly descriptive ethnographic account of his ten years of participant observation in two women's shelters in the Washington, D.C., area, notes major differences. One shelter, he calls "The Refuge" was staffed mostly by volunteers, and was housed in the fellowship hall of a church. It was a "low-demand" (for the shelter users) albeit bare-bones shelter. Liebow found that women appeared to be comfortable there, despite the physical limitations of the space. On the other hand, "The Bridge" was conceptualized as a therapeutic house, providing shelter for women, but with the understanding that the women would be actively working on a case plan to return to permanent housing. The staff was paid and well educated, and, according to Liebow's observations, were more burned out than the volunteer staff of "The Refuge." In his work, Liebow became the conduit for illustrating the hard work and courage of women living in both shelters as they faced life with limited resources and little family support. The book, *Tell Them Who I Am*, was written in part in collaboration with the homeless women and staff of the two shelters, who read and commented on the manuscript. Liebow prints this commentary on his insights in footnotes which occur throughout the book. His is one of the few works in contemporary anthropology which takes the idea of collaboration with the community under study seriously and literally.

In their work in New York City, Baxter and Hopper found that in addition to the city-owned or contracted shelter beds, there were mission shelters (see Jacqueline Wiseman's now classic study, *Stations of the Lost* for a description of Salvation Army–type shelters) and what Baxter and Hopper term Digger-type missions, where staff live with the homeless and create a community with them. "Digger" refers to a sixteenth-century utopian communal group opposed to private property (Baxter and Hopper 1981: 68). Another tradition of sheltering the homeless arose with the Catholic Worker movement of Dorothy Day, in which, ideally, worker and resident live together as equals (Roberts 1984). According to Baxter and Hopper, these shelters or enclaves are extremely popular and are often full.

Doubling-Up

Probably the least researched type of adaptation to homelessness is that of living with another family, usually another poor family, on a very temporary basis. This is referred to as "doubling-up" and is often a precursor to life on the streets, or in encampments and shelters.

In Janet Fitchen's pioneering work on rural homelessness in New York state (1991a, 1991b, and 1996), she found that the most frequent form of lack of adequate shelter among the rural poor was to squeeze two families into a trailer or apartment that was already too small for one. These arrangements were often short-lived, as the strain of the situation made life unbearable. Fitchen found that doubling-up was associated not with mental illness or substance abuse, but a worsening economy in rural areas due to the great loss of manufacturing jobs. Another factor that led to doubling-up was the rise of single motherhood in which income (through work or welfare) was not adequate to pay rent. Fitchen also observed that there was much "hidden homelessness" in rural areas. Women, for example, stay with boyfriends or let them stay in their apartments even if they no longer like them as a way to share the cost of rent. Homelessness in rural areas, then, is especially difficult to count, since these periods of being doubled-up are short-lived, with frequent moves between family and friends. A pattern was for a family to rent a trailer or apartment that they clearly could not afford, and then move into a doubled-up situation when they were forced to leave the rental.

Anna Lou Dehavenon (1996) also has documented the relationship between doubling-up and homelessness through her work in New York City's Emergency Assistance Units (EAUs) program, which receives homeless families and places them in temporary shelters. One issue that emerged from her studies was the policy of sending homeless families back into doubled-up situations, which 78 percent of the families had just come from (Dehavenon 1996: 57). Dehavenon poses the question: to what extent do doubled-up situations allow families to fulfill their domestic needs such as nutrition, privacy for husband and wife, and the ability to communicate with the outside world (e.g., receive phone calls and mail)? Dehavenon found that despite the fact that 92 percent of the guest families paid the host families rent money, the guest families were not able to live as a family in these severely overcrowded conditions.

Dehavenon's work is important in several ways. One is that she interviewed the homeless families utilizing a rigorously obtained random sample taken from among families waiting to be served in the Emergency Assistance Units. Also, she presented her results to the press and to city agencies in such a way that they could not ignore her findings and recommendations. And finally, Dehavenon has been documenting the situation of homeless families in New York City for more than a decade and so can comment on the long-term effects on homeless families of various city policies.

The Future

In light of this array of descriptions of adaptations to a lack of shelter, what is the future of homelessness research? One critical question about many of these ethnographic studies is, as rich as they are, how many have been translated into action? Have shelters, for example, modified their programs in the face of analyses of the effects of stultifying and controlling atmospheres? Have the daily rounds of the homeless, as they visit soup kitchens, collect cans, and "pass" as travelers in an airport been taken into account when designing services for the homeless? Or has this research, when it *has* been mentioned, even fleetingly, simply added "local color" (to use Hopper's term) to a larger report?

The next chapter reviews some of the efforts to help people move toward stable situations. Some of the most effective programs and services have been informed by accounts of the rhythms of life of those on the street.

Chapter 5

Pathways Out of
Homelessness

What do we know about ending homelessness? If many of the homeless shelters of the U.S. and Canada have not been effective in leading people to permanent housing, what programs and strategies have proven helpful? How has the voluminous research on the cultures of the homeless been translated into action that leads to secure housing?

In an effort to disseminate information about some of the world's exemplary programs, we will here review the outcomes of several of the most interesting and effective projects that have made a positive impact on the lives of the homeless.

Outreach

An early step in what might be thought of as the re-housing or resettlement of people living out-of-doors involves offering social contact, referrals, and advocacy (all trying to lead up to permanent housing) to a portion of the visibly homeless. An interesting example of outreach work and its subsequent evaluation was the Park Homeless Outreach Project in New York

City (Ukeles Associates 1995). Here teams of workers became acquainted with the homeless men, women, and couples who occupied three Manhattan parks, one of which (the Carl Schurz) also houses Gracie Mansion, the Mayor's official residence. The outreach teams had contact with 283 different individuals, and they connected eighty-nine of the people to services such as detoxification and substance-abuse treatment, entitlement programs, and temporary shelters. They placed twenty-four clients into permanent or transitional housing (Ukeles Associates 1995: 2). The outreach teams were especially effective in making contact with almost every homeless park dweller, as illustrated below:

> In March 1993, C.K. was living in a storage room under one of the ramps onto the F.D.R. Drive. When a major blizzard hit, the Team did not see C.K. for several days, and began to worry that he may not have survived the extreme weather. The Parks worker coordinated her efforts to find C.K. with the 19th Precinct, Project HELP, and other members of Lenox Hill's pre-existing outreach team. He was located in his "room." (Ukeles Associates 1995: 48)

The project was much less successful in linking individuals to permanent housing: after six months in placement, only *three* of the twenty-four park dwellers placed in housing were known to be still sleeping indoors. Nevertheless, there are many lessons learned in this outreach project about the types of skills required by staff and the kinds of activities that are effective in making initial contact with people whose lives are conducted out-of-doors. For example, it was important for an individual outreach worker to concentrate on a very specific geographical location in the park, in order for trusting relationships to develop. The worker needed to have regular hours in the park, but also be able to be flexible and come to the park as needed. Cellular phones helped the outreach workers link the client directly and immediately with service providers when they were ready to move forward in their steps to re-housing. Once the clients were housed it was important for the outreach worker to stay in touch with them, and find new housing if the first placements did not work out.

The Service Hub

The service hub, as a strategy to provide assistance to the homeless, grew from the research of geographers Michael Dear, Jennifer Wolch, and Robert Wilton (1994), who documented the importance of social networks for people on the street. The service hub situates an array of already existing or newly created services near each other so that someone can readily obtain help in maintaining an independent life (Dear, Wolch, and Wilton 1994: 188). The services may include shelters, day centers, soup kitchens, community health and mental health centers, financial assistance, educational and employment services. In order not to "ghettoize" human services in the downtown areas of cities, the authors advocate decentralizing the service hubs so that they exist in metropolitan areas, small towns, and rural areas. The person who becomes service-dependent should not have to travel to the city (and probably end up staying there) in order to access services. The hubs themselves should consist of relatively small agencies and services that capitalize on the existing "folk support" systems already in place. Finally, the service hubs should be as aesthetically pleasing as possible and take into account any deterrents (such as the threat of crime) that would discourage anyone from coming to the hub to seek assistance.

Utilizing the Indigenous Leadership in Homeless Communities

There are many examples of leadership and social support among homeless people, whether they are in encampments, single-room-occupancy hotels, or shelters. These examples can prefigure projects that seek to provide permanent and safe housing for the homeless.

Joan Shapiro (1969) documented the dominant leaders within three different single-room-occupancy hotels. All three were women who were able to provide emotional and material aid to the other hotel residents. They were also able to be a link to the professionals who came to the hotel to provide health and social services. Almost twenty years later, Glasser (1988) documented the social networks and leadership exhibited within the dining room of a soup kitchen. The leaders among the soup kitchen guests were seen as *more* effective at sharing information and making referrals than was the staff. A program that taught accurate information about community resources to groups of soup-kitchen leaders, who were chosen from the various social networks within the dining room, appeared to be effective in increasing the fund of knowledge of these leaders.

Daytime Respites

While on the street, there is an intermediate step of service between outreach efforts and permanent shelter which may be termed a "daytime respite," or a place of rest and refuge for the homeless person. One of the most successful daytime respites we have seen is Chez Doris, a multilingual (French, English, and increasingly, Inuktitut, the language of the Inuit) daytime shelter for women in Montreal (Chez Doris 1992). The center was named after Doris, a destitute young woman who was murdered on the street in 1974. Chez Doris is the gathering spot for over sixty women a day; they come for food, clothing, baths, laundry facilities, and most of all, the companionship of the other women and the staff. The center is funded by a combination of government and private donations, and the women who utilize Chez Doris also provide much of the labor needed to run the place. It is a "low demand, no-questions-asked" service that accepts women who are poor, on the street, and may have psychiatric and/or substance-abuse problems. In one year (1993), over 2000 women used the center (Chez Doris 1994).

The "community living room" of the Berkeley Support Services of Berkeley, California provides a similar opportunity for the homeless poor to socialize (Segal and Baumohl 1985). The community living room offers people a place to be (to "hang out"), a place to connect with survival services (e.g., financial assistance), a point of contact for mental health and case man-

Photos 5.1 and 5.2 Chez Doris, a daytime respite for women in Montreal (Photos by André Costopoulos)

agement services, and food and shelter. The community living room concept incorporates the culture and worldview of the contemporary chronically mentally ill:

> Today's chronic patients also represent a generation of mental health clients who are young (average age about thirty-five years) and whose relationship with institutions has been formed in an era of civil rights and consumerism. Few have experienced long-term hospitalization, and few exhibit the apathy, lack of initiative, or the resignation that numerous studies found to characterize the long-term mental hospital resident. These "new" chronic patients have not been socialized to docility, to the role of acquiescent mental patient; they do not use services in the tractable fashion of their predecessors but rather as wary, often angry consumers demanding response to their broad needs for social and economic support. (Segal and Baumohl 1985: 112)

Rather than approaching the users of the community living room as mentally ill, clients, or subjects of charity, Segal and Baumohl advocate that workers and users of such services engage in a process of "mutual disclosure" (Segal and Baumohl 1985: 114). The details of how the process may be facilitated are not, however, described in their published work.

A final example of a "no-questions-asked" daytime respite is El Patio, a community program for street children including play, laundry services, and food in Bogotá, Colombia (Goode 1987a). This program represents a first step in a series of programs that emphasize education for occupations (including "street" occupations that the children are already doing) and self-government. Unlike many other street schools (as they are often called) in the developing world, the emphasis is *not* on reuniting children with their families, who are seen as having had to give up their children to the streets due to severe poverty. In an excellent review of the details of El Patio and its related programs, Judith Goode (1987a) discusses the tensions that exist between philosophies of love and nurturing needed by the children and the desire to push them into adult-style self-sufficiency. She also discusses the different orientations of staff members. Some are involved in this work because of their religious beliefs, some are former street children themselves, others are professionals and members of the middle and upper classes, while still others are university students. Goode views former street children as among the most effective staff members and as having the longest-term commitment.

Case Management

When working with homeless people in outreach efforts, day respites, and shelters, one service generally offered is that of *case management*. In one of the few detailed studies documenting *what* case management services *are*, Céline Mercier and Guylaine Racine (1995) analyze the daily contacts log of two case managers serving twenty-five homeless and formerly homeless (but still not permanently housed) women affiliated with Maison l'invitée, a detoxification and rehabilitation center for substance-abusing homeless women in Montreal, Quebec. The case management activities for the twenty-five women took place in the community, out of an office (which was in fact an apartment in downtown Montreal) over a period of three years.

There were 11,104 contacts with the twenty-five women analyzed in this research project. The contacts lasted an average of 24.3 minutes, and the median number of contacts for each woman was 16.3. Two-thirds of all the contacts focused on support (building and maintaining relationships and encouraging the woman) and money management. In addition, twenty-two of the women received help with their housing (Mercier and Racine 1995: 30).

There are two interesting observations from this Montreal study. One is that the homeless women who entered the program during the third year of operation had, overall, less contact with the case managers than the women who were involved in the first two years of the study. Mercier and Racine hypothesize that the case managers were so involved with the clients of the first two years, many of whose lives were in crisis, that they could not really give the same attention to the third-year group. Additionally, the authors were surprised at how few contacts (19.9 percent) took place outside of the office (e.g., on the street, in a soup kitchen, or in the woman's room). The authors suggest that perhaps the workers were trying to retain control of their environment in the face of the discouraging situations of their clients, by seeing clients in the office or having only telephone contact. Perhaps a lesson from this study is that even with a "community" orientation, some programs revert to the more traditional office setting unless conscious steps are taken to keep this from happening.

Transitional and Supportive Housing

In the United States, by the mid-1980s, a pattern was developing in which at least some of the homeless population experienced *repeated* episodes of shelter living. Many people were not able to make the transition from shelter to apartment living and were in need of a lot more support in order to maintain permanent housing. In the United States, the Department of Housing and Urban Development (HUD) as well as non-governmental community development organizations began funding housing strategies that supported the homeless in their quest for housing. These strategies, which are still used today, include transitional housing, generally consisting of housing with two years of services; and supportive housing, which is housing with the provision of services for an open-ended period of time. Transitional and supportive housing may be provided in one physical space (e.g., apartments built in former factories, such as Ma Chambre in Montreal, or My Sister's Place in Hartford), or it may be provided in scattered apartments in publicly or privately owned buildings, with services brought in to individuals or families. In many communities, transitional and supportive housing is much preferred over building more shelters, which are often viewed with fear and suspicion. Increasingly, it is also being recognized that transitional and supportive housing models may offer far more economical options than emergency shelters or institutions such as psychiatric hospitals or detention centers (Mayor's Homelessness Action Task Force 1998:43).

An interesting approach to transitional housing is finding foster families for homeless families. This has been carried out in St. Paul, Minnesota, through the Human Service Associates (HAS), a private, nonprofit, child-placing agency (Cornish 1992). Utilizing their experience in providing foster care to children, and noting the lack of social support and sense of isolation that was found in the research on homeless families (e.g., Bassuk, Rubin, and Lauriat 1986), HAS placed thirty-four families with host families. In an evaluation of the project from 1989 to 1991, Cornish found that 60 percent of the foster families co-resided with the host family for a period of four to six months, moved into their own housing, and were still in their own housing six months later (1992:56). The host families were paid $850 per month for housing the homeless family. They received twenty-four hours of training the first year, eighteen hours the second year, and ongoing training and support. Some of the best host families were those who had themselves overcome poverty, abuse, and/or chemical dependence, and were very familiar with the community resources of their neighborhoods.

In Montreal, supportive housing, through the FOHM (La Fédération des OSBL [(Organismes Sans But Lucratif)] d'Habitation de Montréal), provides 1000 tenants with ongoing help in the form of social workers, referrals to health and social-service agencies, tenant organizations, and recreational activities to ensure that high-risk tenants (e.g., the chronically mentally ill) will be successful in *keeping* their housing. The housing is affordable (defined in Canada as being no more than 30 percent of a person's income). A key component of supportive housing is the role of the onsite *concierge*, whose services are integral to the stability of the tenants' lives (FOHM 1997). Research conducted by a team from the University of Quebec in Montreal, who closely interviewed a sample of thirty-three FOHM tenants, concluded that there were significant improvements in the tenants' overall quality of life, and that the tenants expressed a high degree of satisfaction with their housing. The researchers conclude: "It is now easier for these marginalized people to develop friendships because they feel more on the same level as the other tenants and no longer looked on as 'the fool on the block...'" (FOHM 1997:14).

An important issue in the development of alternatives to shelter living is the cost of the housing. The physical renovation of old hotels and factories is expensive. However, if a nonprofit corporation is in charge, the future costs of administering housing at these renovated sites appears to be less expensive to the individual resident (through money from work or from an assistance program) than paying for a room at a commercial SRO. For instance, in the case of newly renovated SRO hotels in New York City, the cost of housing managed by nonprofit agencies (paid for by social assistance) is $10,000 a year, in contrast to $19,000 to $20,000 for a commercial SRO or a shelter (Hamm 1997).

Homesteading

As in the pioneer frontier days of the United States and Canada, urban homesteading represents one strategy for providing housing, when homeless people take over abandoned buildings and try to claim them as their own. An example of contemporary homesteading is Harding Park, located on the waterfront in the Bronx, New York, a twenty-acre community which now has 250 small homes on it. The area had been a weekend campsite for apartment dwellers since the early 1900s (Alvarez 1996). The story of Harding Park is one of working class, mostly Puerto Rican, residents living in high-crime neighborhoods in the Bronx, who found a tract of dilapidated shacks at the water's edge. The area was reminiscent of the fishing villages of Puerto Rico. They moved in and, through their own labor and materials, turned the shacks into habitable houses. Mayor Edward I. Koch took the unusual step of exempting the shacks from municipal building codes. In 1982, after many years of negotiations with the city of New York, the deed for the land was turned over to the residents' association.

Another example of the potential in homesteading is the conversion of a formerly derelict convent in Williamsburg, Brooklyn, into a cooperative apartment building (Rozhon 1996). In a situation similar to the Harding Park example, a group of people whose previous housing was precarious (though none were literally homeless) became attached to a particular location – in this case, one with the aesthetic appeal of a stately historic building. After years of complicated financial and legal battles, the homesteaders were able to purchase their own apartments at prices low-income people could afford.

Self-Help Housing

Self-help housing is a general rubric which has been applied to many strategies that capitalize on the leadership and labor of the future residents. The term may be applied to self-built housing for the working and middle class, such as the People's Self-Help Housing Corporation of San Luis Obispo, California (Newman 1997), or to the World Bank-sponsored upgrades of squatter settlements in the Third World (Keare and Parris 1982). As self-help housing applies to homeless communities, we will look at three self-help programs from Toronto, Canada, each of which directly involves members of homeless communities.

StreetCity in Toronto is a nonprofit pilot housing project that has been developed in direct consultation with the chronically homeless (Anderson 1997, Bridgman 1998s, 1998b). Residents include the literally homeless who have lived on the street, as well as those who have circulated from shelter to shelter or have been barred from shelters. StreetCity occupies a vacant warehouse originally owned by the city and then transferred to the province. The renovation and construction costs for the project were approximately half a million dollars. This created transitional housing for seventy chronically homeless single men and women. Funding for capital costs came from many levels of provincial, metropolitan, and municipal governments.

The project grew from an idea generated by a group of homeless and formerly homeless men and hostel workers. The facility first opened in December 1988 while still under construction and operated as a hostel dormitory with forty homeless men sleeping on the second floor. Some of the men worked as laborers on the construction crew. This kind of incremental building, in which housing may be partially occupied while still

Photo 5.3 Looking down the "Main Street" in StreetCity (Toronto)
(Photo by Rae Bridgman)

under construction, required a relaxation of municipal and provincial building standards.

StreetCity was developed as supportive housing, staffed twenty-four hours a day (with at least two staff on duty), seven days a week, to help residents in developing a co-operative and mutual-help approach to their personal and group needs. While initially designed as transitional housing (a stepping stone to more independent conventional housing), the facility in fact became home for many of its residents. StreetCity is funded through a combination of governmental hostel payments and monthly rents paid by the residents.

Over time, StreetCity residents developed an elaborate community structure including a biweekly meeting of residents, known as Town Council, with an elected mayor and mayoress. A mediation committee helps to resolve conflicts, and a maintenance crew handles care taking and building repair. An intake committee composed of residents and staff reviews applications from homeless people who want to come and live in the building. Once someone has indicated their interest in moving to Street-City (perhaps through a referral from one of the city's shelters, or by just showing up at the door), that person stays as part of a hostel arrangement for an evaluative period of two weeks.

The fact that there are no curfews at StreetCity, that it is a coed residence, and that drugs and alcohol are not banned in the building as a whole signals the distinct approach that StreetCity has adopted, in direct contrast to the conventional mores of hostel provision in Canada and the United States. Those who began the project recognized that drugs and alcohol are an integral part of street life.

Funding from the province of Ontario to develop a second, more permanent facility modeled after StreetCity and named Strachan House by residents, was received at the beginning of 1995, just before the newly elected conservative provincial government announced massive cutbacks to the Ministry of Housing social-housing programs. While homeless people were not involved in the construction of the building to the same extent they had been for the first StreetCity, a crew of eight homeless and formerly homeless women and men was hired. At the pro-

Photo 5.4 A view of the stairs adjacent to Strachan House's Town Hall (Photo by Robert Burley/Design Archive)

ject's end, two of the women were offered full-time construction positions. Approximately half of StreetCity's residents elected to move to the new project. Renovation of the turn-of-the-century warehouse building cost $3.3 million (Can.). The three-story building has been organized into eleven "houses" under one roof. In keeping with the structure of conventional rooming houses, each tenant has a private bedroom (with refrigerator) and shares a kitchen, bathroom, and common area. Wide public corridors open out to informal common-gathering areas linking the houses. The three floors have been connected vertically at either end of the building by soaring glassed-in atriums. The eastern atrium, designed as the Town Hall, is flanked by the base of a towering chimney.

Operating in part of the same building as Strachan House, but spatially, administratively, and philosophically quite distinct, Savard's is a small pilot project which opened in January of 1997 in order to accommodate ten homeless women, many of whom suffer from severe substance addictions and are identified as having mental-health issues (Bridgman 1999). Savard's was named by the staff after Diane Savard, a woman who survived the streets of Toronto and became a community worker who affected the lives of many others. She died in 1993 at the age of thirty-seven.

Savard's was developed by a group of frontline workers together with the Homes First Society and was originally inspired by the project Women of Hope which was started in 1987 by a group of nuns in Philadelphia (Culhane 1992). The Philadelphia "safe haven" project was reported to have had great success in helping chronically homeless, mentally ill women. Operating funds for Savard's have been received from many levels of government, including the provincial Ministry of Health and private foundations.

Rules at Savard's are few: no violence, no weapons, and no alcohol or illegal drugs. There are no curfews. Savard's is staffed twenty-four hours a day, with two staff on at a time. No one is barred from entry, although some may be asked to "go for a walk" for a period of hours or days should there be some provocation. There is no time limit; no rent or other fee is charged.

Photo 5.5 One of the communal kitchens in Strachan House (Photo by Robert Burley/Design Archive)

Should a woman decide to leave Savard's, her bed will be held for her for a period of two weeks after last contact (contact can include a phone call). Women are not required to take medication, and referrals are made only when a woman has herself indicated interest. Assurance of food and shelter is offered without being tied to mandatory substance-abuse treatment programs or other social services.

The examples provided by StreetCity and Strachan House provide us with alternatives to many institutional shelter facilities for chronically homeless women and men. They utilize the competence of street people to help in the design, development, and maintenance of their housing. They also provide citizenship rights, of which many street people have been disenfranchised, through a system of self-governance. Examples such as Savard's show the potential for granting homeless people, even those with histories of distress, a secure place to live. The Toronto models also demonstrate that making vacant municipal buildings available to nonprofit housing initiatives is one way of addressing the needs of homeless people.

Institutionalizing Self-Help Strategies

The self-help approach has been used in many countries and in many forms. An interesting institutionalization of the concept is found in Cuba, especially during the decade of the 1970s, when 80,000 dwellings were built by the *microbrigadas*, groups of workers from factories or offices whose labor was redirected toward building shelter for themselves and their colleagues. In a review of this nationwide experience of self-help in housing, Kosta Mathéy (1988) presents the successes of these housing teams, and contrasts the quality and efficiency of their work to a later effort in Cuba when it met its housing needs through Ministry of Construction workers. So successful were the *microbrigadas*, that Fidel Castro reinstituted them in the 1980s. An important reason why the apartment buildings constructed by the *microbrigadas* were not looked on as ghettos (despite some physical monotony) was that those who now lived in them had been involved in their construction. In the United States and Canada, projects such as Habitat for Humanity utilizes teams of volunteers (including prospective residents) to build housing and renovate old units. However, this kind of communal effort occurs on a very limited basis.

Cohousing

Cohousing is a concept in housing design in which a maximum sense of community is gained while the immediate family still retains privacy. Most often, cohousing refers to multifamily dwellings with shared facilities such as playrooms, guest bedrooms, entertainment areas, laundry, sewing rooms, and workshops, with much pedestrian space to encourage social interaction (White-Harvey 1993). Models of cohousing include the long-houses of the Iroquois of the eighteenth and nineteenth centuries (and before) in what is now Canada and the U.S., and the modern *Bofoellesskaber* (living communities) of Denmark. Although not specifically directed to homeless people, aspects of the cohousing philosophy could be adapted to address the problem of social isolation so often felt by the formerly homeless as they move into their own apartments.

In My Sister's Place II in Hartford, Connecticut, the apartments for women and their children in the transitional stage (twenty-four months of residence) were designed for two families: there is a common kitchen and living room, with the bedrooms and bath to the right and left of the common area, in order to give each family unit its own space. This shared housing apparently had limited success (Beaumont 1998), since most of the families wanted an apartment that was totally their own. More research would be valuable for assessing when (and if) cohousing could be utilized for alleviating homelessness.

Other Low-Cost Alternatives

Finally, another means of increasing low-cost housing options is actually to build a house on property obtained by a community organization. Dennis Davies, an architect in Tolland, Connecticut, has designed a single-person 225-square foot house, complete with all amenities, for the purchase price of U.S. $9,950. The house can be added to, and has been considered for disaster-relief housing in Hong Kong and as veteran housing in Brooklyn. The house is low-cost, ensures privacy, and will probably appreciate in value like any standard house (Nieves 1996).

Direct-Access Hostels

Before ending this discussion about the many alternatives to shelter living, it is valuable to ask if at least some of the shelters that offer a "no-questions-asked" direct and easy access to a bed for the night should be kept open. Perhaps by utilizing the

British term *hostel* (meaning inn or hotel) it would be possible to destigmatize the concept of a shelter and consider the functions that shelters now serve.

One group now served by shelters is those who stay for a very short period of time. For example, in research about the pattern use and subsequent closure of the Alvaston Resettlement Unit, a seventy-four-bed shelter in London (Deacon, Vincent, and Walker 1995), it was found that the majority of the men stayed for fewer than four nights. This is also a pattern found in Hartford, Connecticut (Glasser 1996), where 44 percent of the men at the eighty-eight bed McKinney shelter stayed for two weeks or less. The second, though smaller, group of shelter residents are men who have been "on the road" for years, and who want and need the camaraderie and communal living aspects of shelters. In both cases, shelters serve an important function in peoples' lives.

Prevention

A discussion of strategies for housing the homeless would not be complete without some attention to the prevention of homelessness. Since at least a portion of the current homeless population is now chronically homeless, it is important to study what would have prevented them from losing their housing in the first place.

We will here briefly contrast the situations in Canada and the United States in two areas which can prevent homelessness: adequate financial assistance to the very poor and publicly funded housing for the most vulnerable populations. This comparison is based on the work of Glasser, Fournier, and Costopoulos (1999), who have compared homelessness in the two countries.

First, many more people in Canada than in the U.S. are eligible for financial assistance, in part because the definition of "people in poverty" is different in the two societies. The U.S. poverty line is based on a 1964 calculation of need (adjusted for current consumer prices) that is based on the cost of the emergency-food-plan budget. The Canadian low-income cutoff is the average level at which a family spends more than 58.5 percent of its income on food, clothing, and shelter. In 1986, a family of four was considered poor in the U.S. if they had an income of $11.203, while the equivalent low-income cutoff in a large urban area in Canada was $17,330 (expressed in U.S. dollars) (Blank and Hanratty 1993: 200). This means that the eligibility "net" for many types of assistance is considerably wider in Canada, with the result that more money is available for housing for the Canadian poor.

Second, Canada has the concept of *social housing* not found in the U.S. Social housing encompasses public housing, rent subsidies, and supportive housing – all of which help to insure the provision of housing. Ideally, publicly funded housing blends into the surrounding neighborhood, is not cut off from the rest of the community, and is scattered throughout many neighborhoods. Also, there should be enough social housing so that housing is *accessible* to the poorest and most vulnerable groups. Although social housing does exist in the U.S. (even though the term does not), the extent of help with housing appears to have been more generous historically in Canada. Increasingly, however, the provincial and federal governments in Canada have sought to devolve their responsibility for funding social housing initiatives to the municipal level ostensibly as a cost-saving measure.

In Montreal the Office municipal d'habitation de Montréal administers over 19,000 units in 760 sites all over city. Many of these units blend in well architecturally with the surrounding neighborhoods (see photo). Although most of the HLM housing has been provided for families and seniors, housing for groups such as former psychiatric patients has also been developed (Glasser, Fournier, and Costopoulos 1999). In Toronto, one of the earliest housing projects, Regent Park North, in which circulation was cut off from the surrounding streets, is now being redesigned to become better integrated into the surrounding area (Murdie 1997). In the U.S. many of the early large, anonymous, public housing projects have now been abandoned and are being razed.

Anthropologists and others employing long-term research methods have been able to contribute to our knowledge of the intimate workings of measures to alleviate homelessness. Espe-

Photos 5.6 and 5.7 An example of social housing in Montreal, Quebec (Photos by André Costopoulos)

cially exciting is the potential offered in the upgrading of both residential or rezoned industrial structures by future residents themselves, such as in the case of StreetCity. Why have the model projects that have been attempted and proven successful not been more widely emulated? E. Fuller Torrey (1990), a pioneer in work with the homeless mentally ill, reviewed four successful community-based services for the mentally ill, and concluded that they were not replicated (or, in some cases, continued) because of the chaotic funding requirements in the mental-health system. Although the issue of housing homeless people is broader than the mental-health system, we too are challenged to wonder why each city and each community organization appears to have to "reinvent the wheel" when combating homelessness.

Chapter 6

Concluding Thoughts

In the late twentieth century, most social scientists see the evolution of homelessness in terms of the confluence of many factors, only some of which relate to individual misfortunes and pathologies. The best writing on homelessness does not ignore the involvement of drugs, alcohol, prostitution, and mental illness in homeless people's lives, but views these within the broader context of the lack of accessible and affordable housing, the lack of jobs that can sustain individuals and families, society's collusion in letting cities (at least in the U.S.) deteriorate, and the degree to which the state recognizes the importance of a social safety-net for all residents.

The strengths offered specifically by anthropology, which we have highlighted in this book, demonstrate our desire to grasp the world through a "native" point of view, our ability to view problems in a world perspective, our analytical skills for understanding the causes of homelessness, and our disciplinary commitment to long-term and in-depth research. The best ethnographic work avoids romanticized presentations of homeless people while according them respect for their resourcefulness and their attempts to preserve a sense of dignity as they live outside.

It seems to us that the greatest challenge in the anthropology-homelessness endeavor is getting the public to pay serious attention to the research, thereby enabling anthropologists to become part of dialogues for social change. It appears that, with several exceptions, anthropological research on homelessness has been relegated to the sidelines of public-policy discussions, adding only colorful descriptions of people on the streets. Why do the general public and policymakers in North America not look to anthropology for a leadership role?

One explanation is that anthropologists are not generally thought of as providing the concrete numbers viewed as necessary in any analysis of a social problem. While many anthropologists have indeed been interested in documenting the extent and nature of homelessness, others, such as sociologists and epidemiologists, are more often considered first. Similarly, in analyzing the causes of homelessness, the expertise of psychologists and psychiatrists has been sought in order to discuss the role of mental illness in homelessness research. The fields of economics, urban planning, and political science have dominated discussions of the economic and political background of homelessness.

A potential model for anthropology's relationship to homelessness is offered by the discipline's leadership in research on the AIDS epidemic. Here, it seems, anthropology is well regarded for having unearthed modes of transmission, and for pointing the way to effective, culturally congruent public-health initiatives that seek to prevent the spread of HIV infection (e.g., Singer and Weeks 1996; Feldman and Johnson 1986; Farmer 1992). Perhaps AIDS has riveted the attention of all social classes and political leaders, so that there is an urgency to the topic that homelessness, as a visible reminder of poverty, does not have. Perhaps the funding sources for anthropology in AIDS studies are agencies (such as the Center for Disease Control) that more expertly disseminate the results of research.

One of the most important lessons from AIDS research has been the use of participatory research that involves the communities under study. For example, in recent work on designing and evaluating HIV/AIDS prevention work in Hartford, Connecticut, the Hispanic Health Council (see Singer and Marxuach-

Rodriguez 1996) formed the Latino Gay Men's Health Project, which reached gay Latino men, a group missed by previous prevention efforts. The level of detail of cultural knowledge about the many subgroups that exist within the general rubric of Latino men who have sex with other men, and the kinds of public-health strategies that will be effective with each group, make this piece of anthropological research extremely valuable.

Similarly, it is important to emphasize the potential of participatory research on homelessness, which enables the homeless to have an active voice in the development, design, and operation of housing and other initiatives suitable to their needs. An example of participatory research we have discussed is the work of Elliot Liebow, who collaborated with a group of homeless women in order to effectively present the details of their lives. He also outlined the conditions that would be necessary to end their homelessness. Participatory research could extend to the evaluation of projects or initiatives that seem to be working well in efforts to end homelessness.

Further, well-timed publicity, as is represented by Anna Lou Dehavenon's (1995) yearly reports and press conferences about family homelessness in New York City, communicates the results of research findings to the press, politicians, agency directors, and community activists. Another avenue of dissemination that makes our research heard is working closely with advocacy groups, some of whom may directly sponsor our research. Merrill Eisenberg (1994) points out that in her experience, the commitment of the sponsoring agency is *the* crucial factor in translating research into policy.

We could learn more from successful projects and programs to end homelessness. Overall, initiatives to end homelessness would benefit from more systematically conducted evaluation that could offer future efforts more concrete guidance in the strengths and weaknesses inherent in various strategies. Further, we could do more to extend the study of homelessness to the study of the vast network of service providers, a network which is at times sardonically referred to as "the shelter industry." It is the people of this network who daily influence the quality of life of the homeless and who are looked upon by the public at large as the main source of knowledge about homelessness. The cultural assumptions of our public policymakers and politicians should more often be the focus of study, as collective action affects the quality of life for society's most vulnerable members.

Despite anthropology's historical legacy of cross-cultural research, the study of homelessness outside the United States and Canada has not been fully considered by anthropologists. We know from many examples that the cross-cultural lens enables us to focus on the inherent assumptions that cloud our thinking when we are confronted with problems in our own society.

Finally, so much of the work that anthropologists have done has involved the "lone researcher" paradigm. We feel that there are missed opportunities for anthropologists to share our hard-won knowledge of the streets with research teams and community organizations which are working to alleviate the plight of the homeless. Anthropology has historically drawn together diverse approaches under its umbrella. We are well equipped from our training to take on research that requires interdisciplinary breadth and the flexibility to synthesize and communicate multiple, and at times, competing, perspectives.

Bibliography

Alvarez, Lizette. 1996. "A Neighborhood of Homesteaders." *The New York Times* (31 December): A14.

Anderson, Rae (also known as Rae Bridgman). 1996 "Integrating Residence and Work in Building Codes in Canada." *Open House International* 21(2): 41-48.

_____. 1997. "The Street as Metaphor in Housing for the Homeless." *The Journal of Social Distress and the Homeless* 6(1): 1-12.

Aubry, Tim, Shawn Currie, and Celine Pinsent. 1996. Development of a Homeless Data Collection and Management System: Phase One. Ottawa: Social and Economic Policy and Research Division.

Baker, Susan Gonzalez. 1994. "Gender, Ethnicity, and Homelessness." *American Behavioral Scientist* 37(4): 476-504.

Balmori, Diana and Margaret Morton. 1993. *Transitory Gardens, Uprooted Lives.* New Haven and London: Yale University Press 1994.

Bascom, Jonathan. 1993 "'Internal Refugees': The Case of the Displaced in Khartoum." In *Geography and Refugees: Patterns and Processes for Change,* ed. Richard Black and Vaughan Robinson, 33-46. London: Belhaven Press.

Bassuk, Ellen L. 1993. "Social and Economic Hardships of Homeless and Other Poor Women." *American Orthopsychiatric Association, Inc.* 63(3): 340-347.

Bassuk, Ellen L., Lenore Rubin, and Alison Lauriat. 1986. "Characteristics of Sheltered Homeless Families." *American Journal of Public Health* 76(9): 1097-1101.

Bassuk, Ellen L. and John C. Buchner. 1997. "Homelessness in Female-Headed Families: Childhood and Adult Risk Factors." *American Journal of Public Health* 87(2): 241-248.

Baxter, Ellen and Kim Hopper. 1981. *Private Lives/Public Spaces: Homeless Adults on the Streets of New York City.* New York: Community Service Society.

Beaumont, Judith. 1998. Personal Communication with Director, My Sister's Place, Hartford, Connecticut, 15 March.

Beavis, Mary Ann, Nancy Klos, Tom Carter, and Christian Couchant. 1997. Literature Review: Aboriginal Peoples and Homelessness. Ottawa: Canada Mortgage and Housing Corporation.

Behr, Michelle and Patricia Gober. 1982. "When a Residence Is Not a Home: Examining Residence-Based Migration Definitions." *Professional Geographer* 34(2): 178-184.

Benda, Brent B. 1990. "Crime, Drug Abuse, and Mental Illness: A Comparison of Homeless Men and Women." *Journal of Social Science Research* 13(3): 39-60.

Blank, Rebecca M. and Maria J. Hanratty. 1993. "Responding to Need: A Comparison of Social Safety Nets in Canada and the United States." In *Small Differences That Matter: Labor Markets and Income Maintenance in Canada and the United States*, eds. David Card and Richard B. Freeman, 191-231. Chicago: The University of Chicago Press.

Bobiwash, A. Rodney. 1997. "Native Urban Self-Government in Toronto and the Politics of Self-Determination. In *The Meeting Place: Aboriginal Life in Toronto* eds. Frances Sanderson and Heather Howard-Bobiwash, 84-94. Toronto: Native Canadian Centre of Toronto.

Bodley, John H. 1996. *Anthropology and Contemporary Human Problems*, 3rd ed. Mountain View, California: Mayfield Publishing Company.

Borofsky, Robert. 1994. "Introduction." In *Assessing Cultural Anthropology*, ed. Robert Borofsky, 1-28. New York: McGraw-Hill, Inc.

Boone, Margaret S. 1987. "Inner-City Black Undercount: An Exploratory Study on the Causes of Coverage Error." *Evaluation Review* 11(2): 216-241.

Boudimbou, Guy. Charlotte Biederman, trans. 1992. "Les immigrés africains et le squatt des logements sociaux dans la région parisienne." Paper given at the Fifth International Research Conference on Housing, Montréal, Québec, July 7-10.

Bourgois, Philippe. 1995. In *Search of Respect: Selling Crack in El Barrio*. Cambridge: Cambridge University Press.

Breakey, W.R., P.J. Fischer, M. Kramer, G.N. Nestadt, A.J. Romanoski, A. Ross, R.M. Royall, and O.C. Stine. 1989. "Health and Mental Health Problems of Homeless Men and Women in Baltimore." *Journal of the American Medical Association* 262: 1352-1357.

Brettell, Caroline B. 1996a. "Migration." *Encyclopedia of Cultural Anthropology*, vol. 3, 793-801. New York: Henry Holt and Company.

_____ 1996b. *When They Read What We Write: The Politics of Ethnography*. Westport, Connecticut: Bergin & Garvey.

Bridgman, Rae (also known as Anderson). 1996. Excerpt of an Interview at StreetCity.

_____. 1998a. "The Architecture of Homelessness and Utopian Pragmatics." *Utopian Studies* 9(1):50-67.

_____. 1998b. "A 'City' Within the City: A Canadian Housing Model for the Homeless." *Open House International* 23(1):12-21.

_____. 1999 "'Oh, So You Have a Home to Go to?': Empowerment and Resistance in Work with Chronically Homeless Women." In *Fire Under Moss: Feminist Ethnography in Practice*. Co-editors, Rae Bridgman, Sally Cole, and Heather Howard-Bobiwash. Peterborough, Ontario: Broadview Press.

Brown, Susan E. 1977. "Housing in Bogota: A Synthesis of Research and Notes on Anthropological Contributions to the Study of Housing." *Urban Anthropology* 6(3): 249-267.

Burnam, M. Audrey and Paul Koegel. 1988. "Methodology for Obtaining a Representative Sample of Homeless Persons: The Los Angeles Skid Row Study." *Evaluation Review* 12(2): 117-152.

Burns, Leland S. 1988. "Hope for the Homeless in the US: Lessons from the Third World." *Cities* 5(1): 33-40.

Burt, Martha R. 1992. *Over the Edge: The Growth of Homelessness in the 1980's*. New York: Russell Sage Foundation.

Burt, Martha R. and Barbara E. Cohen. 1989. "Differences among Homeless Single Women with Children and Single Men." *Social Problems* (36) 5: 508-524.

Carroll, Barbara Wake. 1995. "Program Drift: The Rational Road to Policy Diversity." *Canadian Journal of Urban Research* 4(1): 21-41.

Chambers, Erve and Setha Low. 1989. "Introduction." In *Housing, Culture and Design: A Comparative Perspective*, eds. Erve Chambers and Setha Low, 3-9. Philadelphia: University of Pennsylvania Press.

Chez Doris. 1994. "The Courier." Newsletter of Chez Doris. Spring.

_____.1992. "Chez Doris: The First Fifteen Years." (Monograph.)

Clifford, J. 1988. *The Predicament of Culture: Twentieth-Century Ethnography, Literature, and Art*. Cambridge, Massachusetts: Harvard University Press.

Clifford, J. and G.E. Marcus, eds. 1986. *Writing Culture: The Poetics and Politics of Ethnography*. Berkeley, California: University of California Press.

Cohen, Carl I. and Jay Sokolovsky. 1989. *Old Men of the Bowery: Strategies for Survival Among the Homeless*. New York: Guildford Press.

Cohen, Carl I., Jeanne Teresi, Douglas Holmes, and Eric Roth. 1988. "Survival Strategies of Older Homeless Men." *The Gerontologist* 28(1): 58-65.

Counts, Dorothy Ayers and David R. Counts. 1996. *Over the Next Hill: RVing Seniors in North America.* Peterborough, Ontario: Broadview Press.

Cornish, Jean. 1992. "Fostering Homeless Children and Their Parents Too: A Unique Approach to Transitional Housing for Homeless Families." *Community Alternatives: International Journal of Family Care* 4(2): 43-59.

Culhane, Dennis P. "Ending Homelessness Among Women with Severe Mental Illness: A Model Program from Philadelphia." *Psychosocial Rehabilitation Journal* 16(1):73-76.

Culhane, Dennis P., Chang-Moo Lee, and Susan M. Wachter. 1996. "Where the Homeless Come From: A Study of the Prior Address Distribution of Families Admitted to Public Shelters in New York City and Philadelphia." *Housing Policy Debate* (7)2: 327-365.

Curtis, Karen. 1996. "Urban Poverty and the Social Provision of Food Assistance." Paper delivered at the Urban Affairs Association Meeting, New York City, April 1996.

Daly, Gerald. 1993. "Place Making by Residents: The Case of Self-help Housing in Canada." *Open House International* 18(1): 20-27.

———— 1996. *Policies, Strategies, and Lives on the Street.* London and New York: Routledge.

Deacon, Alan, Jill Vincent, and Robert Walker. 1995. "Whose Choice, Hostels or Homes? Policies for Single Homeless People." *Housing Studies* 10(3): 345-363.

Dear, Michael, Jennifer Wolch, and Robert Wilton. 1994. *The Service Hub Concept in Human Service Planning*, vol. 42, part 3:174-271. Oxford, England: Pergamon.

Dehavenon, Anna Lou. 1994. "Monitoring Emergency Shelter for Homeless Families in New York City." *Practicing Anthropology* 16(4): 12-16.

————. 1995. "Out in the Cold: The Social Exclusion of New York City's Homeless Families in 1995." (Monograph.) New York: Action Research Project on Hunger, Homelessness, and Family Health.

————. 1996. "Doubling Up and New York City's Policies for Sheltering Homeless Families." In *There's No Place Like Home: Anthropological Perspectives on Housing and Homelessness in the United States*, ed. Anna Lou Dehavenon, 51-66. Westport, Connecticut: Bergin & Garvey.

Desjarlais, Robert. 1994. "Struggling Along: The Possibilities for Experience Among the Homeless Mentally Ill." *American Anthropologist* 96(4): 886-901.

_____ 1996. "Some Causes and Cultures of Homelessness." *American Anthropologist* 98(2): 420-425.

Drakakis-Smith, David. 1987. *The Third World City*. London: Routledge.

Durrenberger, E. Paul. 1996. "Ethnography." *Encyclopedia of Cultural Anthropology*, 416-422. Human Relations Area Files, Inc. and Lakeville, Connecticut: American Reference Publishing Company, Inc.

Dwer, D.J. 1975. *Housing in Third World Cities*. London: Longmans.

Eames, Edwin and Judith Granich Goode. 1997. *Anthropology of the City: An Introduction to Urban Anthropology*. Englewood Cliffs, New Jersey: Prentice-Hall, Inc.

Eisenberg, Merrill. 1994. "Translating Research into Policy: What More Does It Take?" *Practicing Anthropology* 16(4): 35-39.

Epstein, David G. 1972. "The Genesis and Function of Squatter Settlements in Brasilia." In *The Anthropology of Urban Environments*, eds. T. Weaver and D. White, 51-58. Boulder, Colorado: University of California Press.

Evaluation Review 16(4), August 1992 (entire issue).

Fabrega, Horacio Jr. 1971. "Begging in a Southeastern Mexican City." *Human Organization* 303: 277-287.

Farmer, Paul Edward. 1992. *AIDS and Accusation: Haiti and the Geography of Blame*. Berkeley, California: University of California Press.

Farr, R., P. Koegel, and A. Burnam. 1986. *A Study of Homelessness and Mental Illness in the Skid Row Area of Los Angeles*. Los Angeles: Los Angeles County Department of Mental Health.

Feldman, Douglas A. and Thomas M. Johnson. 1986. *The Social Dimension of AIDS Methods and Theory*. New York: Praeger.

Fischer, Pamela J. and William R. Breakey. 1991. "The Epidemiology of Alcohol, Drug, and Mental Disorders Among Homeless Persons." *American Psychologist* 46: 1115-1128.

Fitchen, Janet M. 1991a. *Endangered Space, Enduring Places: Change, Identity, and Survival in Rural America*. Boulder, Colorado: Westview.

_____. 1991b. "Homelessness in Rural Places: Perspectives from Upstate New York." *Urban Anthropology* 20 (2): 177-210.

_____. 1994. "Welfare Reform for Rural America." *Practicing Anthropology* 16(4): 17-22.

_____. 1996. "Rural Upstate New York." In *There's No Place Like Home: Anthropological Perspectives on Housing and Homelessness in the United States*, ed. Anna Lou Dehavenon, 1-17. Westport, Connecticut: Bergin & Garvey.

Flanders, J. 1990. *StreetCity: Homes for the Chronically Homeless*. A Progress Report prepared by John Flanders in association with Jim Ward Associates. Toronto.

FOHM (La Fédération des OSBL [Oganismes Sans But Lucratif] d'Habitation de Montréal). 1997. "Evaluation of Social Housing with Community Support" Roundup Paper-Preliminary Research Results LAREPPS-UQAM, FOHM, CLSC du Plateau Mont-Royal, HQ.

Fournier, Louise. 1988. "Rapport synthèse de l'opération d'énumération de la clientèle des missions et refuges de Montréal." Verdun, Quebec: Centre de Recherche de l'hôpital Douglas.

_____. 1989. "Énumération de la clientèle des missions et refuges de Montréal." Verdun, Quebec: Centre de Recherche de l'hôpital Douglas.

_____. 1991. "Itinérance et santé mentale à Montréal. Étude descriptive de la clientèle des missions et refuges." Verdun, Quebec: Rapport de recherche, Unité de recherche psychosociale, Centre de recherche de l'hôpital Douglas.

Fournier, Louise and Céline Mercier. 1996. *Sans domicile fixe: au-delà du stéréotype.* Montréal: Méridien.

Francis, M. 1989. "Control as a Dimension of Public-Space Quality." In *Public Places and Spaces,* eds. I. Altman and E.H. Zube, 147-172. New York: Plenum Press.

Gates, Hill. 1996. "Political economy." In *Encyclopedia of Cultural Anthropology,* vol. 3, eds. David Levinson and Melvin Ember, 971-975. New York: Henry Holt and Company.

Geertz, Clifford. 1973. *The Interpretation of Cultures.* New York: Basic Books.

Glass, Ruth. 1964. *London: Aspects of Change.* London: Centre for Urban Studies and MacGillion & Kee.

Glasser, Irene. 1988. *More Than Bread: Ethnography of a Soup Kitchen.* Tuscaloosa, Alabama: University of Alabama Press.

_____. 1991. "An Ethnographic Study of Homelessness in Windham, Connecticut." Report #17. Ethnographic Exploratory Research, Center for Survey Methods Research, Bureau of the Census, Washington, D.C.

_____. 1994. *Homelessness in Global Perspective.* New York: G.K. Hall.

_____. 1995. *Urban Life on Film and Video.* Washington, D.C.: Society for Urban Anthropology, American Anthropological Association.

_____. 1996. "Homelessness in Hartford: A Preliminary Study." (Monograph.)

_____. 1997. "A Census of the Homeless in Hartford. (Monograph.)

Glasser, Irene, Louise Fournier, and André Costopoulos. 1999. "Homelessness in Quebec City, Quebec and Hartford, Connecticut: A Cross-National and Cross-Cultural Analysis." Under review.

Gmelch, George. 1985. *Irish Tinkers: The Urbanization of an Itinerant People,* 2nd ed. Prospect Height, Illinois: Waveland Press.

Godelier, Maurice. 1994. "'Mirror, Mirror on the Wall ...' The Once and Future Role of Anthropology: A Tentative Assessment." In *Assessing Cultural Anthropology*, ed. Robert Borofsky, 97-112. New York: McGraw-Hill, Inc.

Goffman, Erving. 1961. *Asylums: Essays on the Social Situation of Mental Patients and Other Inmates*. New York: Anchor Books.

Goode, Judith. 1987a. "Gaminismo: The Changing Nature of the Street Child Phenomenon in Colombia," no. 28. Indianapolis, Indiana: Universities Field Staff International, Inc.

_____. 1987b. "Gaminismo: Recent Trends in Social Programs for Colombian Street Children," no. 29. Indianapolis, Indiana: Universities Field Staff International, Inc.

Gounis, Kostas. 1992. "Temporality and the Domestication of Homelessness." In *The Politics of Time*, ed. Henry I. Rutz, 127-149. Washington D.C.: American Anthropology Association.

Grenell, Peter. 1972. "Planning for Invisible People: Some Consequences of Bureaucratic Values and Practices." In *Freedom to Build: Dweller Control of the Housing Process*, eds. John F.C. Turner and Robert Fichter, 95-121. New York: The Macmillan Company; London: Collier-Macmillan Limited.

Hainer, Peter C. 1985. "Census Definitions and the Politics of Census Information." *Practicing Anthropologist* 7(3): 7-8.

Hamid, Ansley. 1990. "The Political Economy of Crack-Related Violence." *Contemporary Drug Problems* 17(1): 31-78.

Hamm, Lisa M. 1997. "Homeless Find Haven." *The Day* (14 March): D1, D8

Hanssen, Einar. 1996. "Finding Care on the Street: Processes in the Careers of Sri Lankan Street Boys." *Childhood: A Global Journal of Child Research* 3(2): 247-259. (Special Issue on working street children, "Children Out of Place.")

Hardoy, Jorge E. and David Satterthwaite. 1989. *Squatter Citizen: Life in the Urban Third World*. London: Earthscan Publications.

Harrell-Bond, Barbara and Efithia Vourtira. 1996. "Refugees." *Encyclopedia of Cultural Anthropology*, vol. 3. New York: Henry Holt and Company, 1076-1081.

Hauch, Christopher. 1985. Coping Strategies and Street Life: The Ethnography of Winnipeg's Skid Row Region. Report no. 11. Winnipeg, Manitoba: Institute of Urban Studies.

Helleiner, Jane. 1992. The Travelling People: Cultural Identity in Ireland. Ph.D. diss., University of Toronto.

_____. 1997. "Women of the Itinerant Class: Gender and Anti-Traveller Racism in Ireland. *Women's Studies International Forum* 29(2): 1-13.

Hines, Cathy. 1985. "Anthropologists at the Census Bureau." *Practicing Anthropologist* 7(3): 4, 8, 19.

Hopper, Kim. 1988. "More than Passing Strange: Homelessness and Mental Illness in New York City." *American Ethnologist* 15: 155-167.

_____. 1989. "Deviance and Dwelling Space: Notes on the Resettlement of Homeless Persons with Drug and Alcohol Problems." *Contemporary Drug Problems* (Fall): 391-415.

_____. 1990. "Research Findings as Testimony: A Note on the Ethnographer as Expert Witness." *Human Organization* 49(2): 110-113.

_____. 1991. "Symptoms, Survival, and the Redefinition of Public Space: A Feasibility Study of Homeless People at a Metropolitan Airport." *Urban Anthropology* 20(2): 155-175.

_____. 1992. "Counting the Homeless: S-Night in New York." *Evaluation Review* 16(4): 376-388.

_____. 1995. "No Fair Measure: Elliot Liebow's *Tell Them Who I Am* (1993)." Paper presented at a special session of the Annual Meeting of the American Sociological Association, Los Angeles, 6 August 1994.

Hopper, Kim and Jill Hamberg. 1986. "The Making of America's Homeless." In *Critical Perspectives on Housing*, eds. Rachel G. Bratt, Chester Hartman, and Ann Meyerson, 12-40. Philadelphia: Temple University Press.

Hutson, Susan. 1993. Letter to Irene Glasser, 28 January.

Institute of Urban Studies, University of Winnipeg. 1997. "Literature Review: Aboriginal Peoples and Homelessness." Ottawa, Ontario: Canada Mortgage and Housing Corporation.

Jacobs, Jane. 1961. *The Death and Life of Great American Cities*. New York: Vintage Books.

Kalifon, S. Zev. 1989. "Homelessness and Mental Illness: Who Resorts to State Hospitals?" *Human Organization* 48(3): 268-279.

Keare, Douglas H., and Scott Paris. 1982. *Evaluation of Shelter Programs of the Urban Poor: Principle Findings*. World Bank Staff Working Papers. No. 547. Washington, D.C.: The World Bank.

Kearns, R., S.M. Taylor, and M. Dear. 1987. "Coping and Satisfaction Among the Chronically Mentally Ill." *Canadian Journal of Community Mental Health* 6: 13-24.

Kearns, Robin A., Christopher J. Smith, and Max W. Abbott. 1990. "Another Day in Paradise? Life on the Margins in Urban New Zealand." *Social Science and Medicine* 33 (4): 369-379.

Klos, Nancy. 1997. "Research Note: Aboriginal Peoples and Homelessness: Interviews with Service Providers." Canadian Journal of Urban Research 6(1): 40-52.

Koegel, Paul. 1988. *Understanding Homelessness: An Ethnographic Approach*. Los Angeles: Los Angeles Homelessness Project.

_____. 1992. "Through a Different Lens: An Anthropological Perspective on the Homeless Mentally Ill." *Culture, Medicine, and Psychiatry* 16(1): 1-22.

Kramer, B. Josea and Judith C. Barker. 1996. "Homelessness Among Older American Indians, Los Angeles, 1987-1989." *Human Organization* 55: 396-408.

Leda, Catherine, Robert Rosenheck, and Peggy Gallup. 1992. "Mental Illness Among Homeless Female Veterans." *Hospital and Community Psychiatry* 43(10): 1026-1028.

Levinson, David. 1974. "The Etiology of Skid Rows in the United States." *International Journal of Social Psychiatry* 20: 25-33.

Lewis, Oscar. 1961. *Children of Sanchez: Autobiography of a Mexican Family*. New York: Random House.

_____. 1966. *La Vida: A Puerto Rican Family in the Culture of Poverty*. New York: Random House.

Liddiard, Mark and Susan Hutson. 1991. Homeless Young People and Runaways: Agency Definitions and Processes. *Journal of Social Policy* 20(30):365-88.

Liebow, Elliot. 1967. *Tally's Corner: A Study of Negro Streetcorner Men*. Boston: Little, Brown.

_____. 1993. *Tell Them Who I Am: The Lives of Homeless Women*. New York: Penguin Books.

Lloyd, Peter. 1980. *The 'Young Towns' of Lima: Aspects of Urbanization in Peru*. Cambridge, England: Cambridge University Press.

Lovell, A.M. 1984. "Marginality with Isolation: Social Networks and the New Homeless." Paper presented at the 83rd Annual Meeting of the American Anthropological Association, Denver, Colorado, 14-18 November 1984.

Mangin, William P. 1970. *Peasants in Cities: Readings on the Anthropology of Urbanization*. Boston: Houghton Mifflin.

Marshall, Max, Julia Nehring, and Denis Gath. 1994. "Characteristics of Homeless Mentally Ill People Who Lose Contact with Caring Agencies." *Journal of Psychological Medicine* 11(4): 160-163.

Martin, Elizabeth. 1992. "Assessment of S-Night Street Enumeration in the 1990 Census." *Evaluation Review* 16(4): 418-438.

Mathéy, Kosta. 1988. "*Microbrigadas* in Cuba: An Unconventional Response to the Housing Problem in a Latin American State." *Habitat International* 12(4): 55-62.

Mathieu, Arline. 1993. "The Medicalization of Homelessness and the Theater of Repression." *Medical Anthropology Quarterly* 7(2): 170-184.

Maxwell, Andrew H. 1996. "A Home By Any Means Necessary: Government Policy on Squatting in the Public Housing of a Large Mid-Atlantic City." In *There's No Place Like Home: Anthropological Perspectives on Housing and Homelessness in the*

United States, ed. Anna Lou Dehavenon, 67-79. Westport, Connecticut: Bergin & Garvey.

Mayor's Report Homelessness Action Task Force. 1998. *Breaking the Cycle of Homelessness* Interim Report. Toronto, Canada.

McChesney, Kay Young. 1995. "A Review of the Empirical Literature on Contemporary Urban Homeless Families." *Social Service Review,* (September): 429-460.

Mele, Christopher. 1995. "Private Redevelopment and the Changing Forms of Displacement in the East Village of New York." In *Marginal Spaces,* (Comparative Urban and Community Research, vol. 5), ed. Michael Peter Smith, 69-93. New Brunswick, New Jersey: Transaction Publishers.

Mercier, Céline and Guylaine Racine.1995. "Case Management with Homeless Women: A Descriptive Study." *Community Mental Health Journal* 31(1): 25-37.

Morse, Gary A. 1992. "Causes of Homelessness." In *Homelessness: A National Perspective,* eds. M.J. Robert and M. Greenblatt, 3-17. New York: Plenum Press.

Murdie, Robert, et al. 1996. "From Public to Social Housing: Contrasts in Inner-City Toronto." Conference Paper. Urban Affairs Association Annual Meeting. 1-13.

Murray, Harry. 1984. "Time in the Streets." *Human Organization* 43(2): 154-161.

My Home, My Sky. 1990. Directed by Eros Djarot. Asian Pacific Film Tour, East/West Center, Honolulu, Hawaii.

Nanda, Serena. 1991. *Cultural Anthropology.* Belmont, California: Wadsworth.

Nieves, Evelyn. 1996. "Little House on the Market: Homes for Everyman? *New York Times* (24 April): B5.

Nord, Mark and A.E. Luloff. 1996. "Homeless Children and Their Families in New Hampshire: A Rural Perspective. *Social Service Review,* September 1995: 461-478.

North, Carol S. and Elizabeth M. Smith. 1993. "A Comparison of Homeless Men and Women: Different Populations, Different Needs." *Community Mental Health Journal* 29(5): 423-431.

Newman, Morris. 1997. "How Sweet Equity Pays Off in California Housing: Nonprofit Group Helps Buyer Build Home and Save on Labor." *New York Times* (28 September): Real Estate 7.

Novac, Sylvia, Joyce Brown, and Carmen Bourbonnais. 1996. No Room of Her Own: A Literature Review on Women and Homelessness. Ottawa, Canada: Canada Mortgage and Housing Corporation.

Ovrebo, Beverly, Meredith Minkler, and Petra Liljestrand. 1991. "No Room in the Inn: The Disappearance of SRO Housing in the United States." In *Housing Risks and Homelessness among the*

Urban Elderly, ed. Sharon M. Keigher, 77-92. New York: Haworth Press.

Passaro, Joanne. 1996. *The Unequal Homeless: Men on the Street, Women in Their Place*. New York: Routledge.

Patychuk, Dianne, Janet Phillips, and David McKeown. 1996. Excerpts of Draft Report: "Deaths among the Homeless in the City of Toronto, 1979 to 1993." City of Toronto, Department of Public Health.

Peressini, Tracy, Lynn McDonald, and David Hulchanski. 1996. Estimating Homelessness: Towards a Methodology for Counting the Homeless in Canada. Background Report. Prepared for Research Division, Canada Mortgage and Housing Corporation, Ottawa.

Phillips, Amy and Susan Hamilton.1997. "Huts for the Homeless: A Low-Technology Approach for Squatters in Atlanta, Georgia." In *There's No Place Like Home: Anthropological Perspectives on Housing and Homelessness in the United States*, ed. Anna Lou Dehavenon, 81-103. Westport, Connecticut: Bergin & Garvey.

Pierce, Todd G. 1992. "Going Back for the Others: Motivating Movement in the Street Dweller Society." Paper presented at the American Anthropological Association Meeting, San Francisco, California.

Piven, F. and R. Cloward.1971. *Regulating the Poor*. New York: Vintage Books.

Pixote. 1981. Directed by Hector Babenco. EmbraFilms, Burbank, California.

Rappaport, Roy A.1994. "Humanity's Evolution and Anthropology's Future." *Assessing Cultural Anthropology*, ed. Robert Borofsky, 153-167. New York: McGraw-Hill, Inc.

Redick, R. and M. Witkin. 1983. "State and County Mental Hospitals, U.S. 1970-1980 and 1980-1981." Mental Health Statistical Note 169. Rockville, Maryland: National Institute of Mental Health.

Rivlin, Leanne G. 1990. "The Significance of Home and Homelessness." *Marriage and Family Review* 15(102): 39-56.

Rivlin, Leanne G. and Josephine E. Imbimbo. 1989. "Self-help Efforts in a Squatter Community: Implications for Addressing Contemporary Homelessness." *American Journal of Community Psychology* 17(6): 705-728.

Roa, N. Rama. 1992. Letter to I. Glasser, from Deputy Registrar General, Office of the Registrar General, India, 18 March 1992, instructions entitled "Enumeration of Houseless Population and Revisional Round."

Robertson, Marjorie J., Paul Koegel, and Linda Ferguson. 1989. "Alcohol Use and Abuse Among Homeless Adolescents in Hollywood." *Contemporary Drug Problems*, 16(3) Fall, 415-452.

Robertson, Michael Owen. 1991. "Interpreting Homelessness: The Influence of Professional and Non-professional Service Providers." *Urban Anthropology* 29(2): 141-153.

Rosenthal, Rob. 1991. "Straighter From the Source: Alternative Methods of Researching Homelessnesss." *Urban Anthropology* 29(2): 109-126.

Rossi, P.H., J.D. Wright, G.A. Fisher, and G. Willis. 1987. "The Urban Homeless: Estimating Composition and Size." *Science* (March): 1336-1341.

Rouseau, Ann Marie. 1981. *Shopping Bag Ladies: Homeless Women Speak about Their Lives*. New York: Pilgrim Press.

Rozhon, Tracie. 1996. "A Former Convent Becomes a Co-Op," *New York Times* (10 November): Real Estate 6.

Ryle, Gilbert. 1971. *Collected Papers*. New York: Barnes and Noble.

Salaam Bombay. 1986. Directed by Mira Nair. Image Entertainment, Chatsworth, California.

Salo, Matt T. and Pamela Campanelli. 1991. "Ethnographic Methods in the Development of Census Procedures for Enumerating the Homeless." *Urban Anthropology* 20(2): 127-139.

Segal, Steven P. and Jim Baumohl. 1985. "The Community Living Room." *Social Casework* 66(2): 111-116.

Settlements Information Network Africa. 1986. "NGOs and Shelter: Fifteen Case Studies from Africa on Housing and Shelter Programs." Articles from Angola, Botswana, Ghana, Kenya, Malawi, Mozambique, Nigeria, Tanzania, and Zimbabwe. Nairobi: Mazingira Institute.

Shapiro, Joan. 1969. "Dominant Leaders Among Slum Hotel Residents." *American Journal of Orthopsychiatry* 39: 644-50.

Shinn, Marybeth and Beth C. Weitzman. 1990. "Research on Homelessness: An Introduction." *Journal of Social Issues* 46(4): 1-11.

Shostak, Marjorie. 1983. *Nisa: The Life and Words of a !Kung Woman*. New York: Vintage Books.

Singer, Merrill and Luis Marxuach-Rodriguez. 1996. "Applying Anthropology to the Prevention of AIDS: The Latino Gay Men's Health Project." *Human Organization* 55(2): 141-147.

Singer, Merrill and Margaret R. Weeks. 1996. "Preventing AIDS in Communities of Color: Anthropology and Social Prevention." *Human Organization* 55(4): 488-492.

Smiley, Richard. Personal Communication, Mathematical Statistician in the Center for Survey Methods Research, U.S. Bureau of the Census. 6 August 1998.

Smith, Michael Peter, ed. 1995. *Marginal Spaces*. (Comparative Urban and Community Series, vol. 5.) Transaction Publishers.

Snow, D.A. and L. Anderson. 1993. *Down on Their Luck: A Study of Homeless Street People*. Berkeley: University of California Press.

Sosin, Michael, Irving Piliavin, and Herb Westerfelt. 1990. "Toward a Longitudinal Analysis of Homelessness." *Journal of Social Issues* 46(4): 157-174.

Southard, P.A. Dee. 1992. "'Shelters are for Scum, and I Ain't No Bum!': Homeless People Who Avoid Shelters." *California Anthropologist* 18(2): 39-4

_____. 1994. "Forest Families: Homeless Campers Using Public Lands." Paper presented at the Pacific Sociological Association Meeting.

_____. 1996. "Uneasy Sanctuary: Homeless Campers Using Public Lands." Paper delivered at the Pacific Sociological Association Meeting, 22 March, Seattle, Washington.

Spradley, James. 1970. *You Owe Yourself a Drunk: An Ethnography of Urban Nomads*. Boston: Little, Brown.

Stack, Carol. 1974. *All Our Kin: Strategies for Survival in a Black Community*. New York: Harper & Row.

Stark, Louisa R. 1994. "The Shelter as 'Total Institution'." *American Behavioral Scientist* 37(4): 553-562.

Sterk-Elifson, Claire and Kirk W. Elifson. 1992. "Someone to Count on: Homeless, Male Drug Users and Their Friendship Relations." *Urban Anthropology* 21(3): 235-251.

Stern, Mark J. 1984. "The Emergence of the Homeless as a Public Problem." *Social Service Review* (June): 291-301.

Stoner, Madeleine R. 1989. *Inventing a Non-Homeless Future: A Public Policy Agenda for Preventing Homelessness*. Series 11, Anthropology and Sociology, vol. 29. New York: Peter Lang.

Struening, Elmer L. and Deborah K. Padgett. 1990. "Physical Health Status, Substance Use and Abuse, and Mental Disorders among Homeless Adults." *Journal of Social Sciences* 46(4): 65-81.

Susser, Ida. 1993. "Creating Family Forms: The Exclusion of Men and Teenage Boys from Families in the New York City Shelter System, 1987-91." *Critique of Anthropology* 13(3): 267-283.

_____. 1996. "The Construction of Poverty and Homelessness in U.S. Cities." *Annual Review of Anthropology* 25: 411-435.

Tierney, John. 1996. "Save the Flophouse." *New York Times Magazine* (14 January): 16.

Tomas, Anna and Helga Dittmar. 1995. "The Experience of Homeless Women: An Exploration of Housing Histories and the Meaning of Home." *Housing Studies* 10(4): 493-515.

Toro, Paul A., Edison J. Trickett, David D. Wall, and Deborah A. Salem. 1991. "Homelessness in the United States: An Ecological Perspective." *American Psychologist* 46: 1208-1218.

Torrey, Fuller E. 1990. "Economic Barriers to Widespread Implementation of Model Programs for the Seriously Mentally Ill." *Hospital and Community Psychiatry* 41(5): 526-531.

Turner, Bertha, ed. 1988. "Building Community: A Third World Case Book." A Summary of the Habitat International Coalition Non-Governmental Organization's Project for the International Year of Shelter for the Homeless, 1987, in association with Habitat Forum Berlin. (Monograph.)

Turner, John. 1976. *Housing by the People: Towards Autonomy in Building Environments*. London: Marion Boyars.

Ukeles Associates Inc. 1995. "Evaluation of the Park Homeless Outreach Project Report to the New York Community Trust." New York City.

UNICEF. Executive Board, 1986. Exploitation of Working Children and Street Children. In Gary Barker and Felicia Knaul 1991, *Exploited Entrepreneurs: Street and Working Children in Developing Countries* (page 2). New York: CHILDHOPE-USA.

U.S. Department of Commerce, Bureau of the Census. 1990a. "Fact Sheet for 1990 Decennial Census Counts of Persons in Selected Locations Where Homeless Persons are Found." Washington, D.C.

_____. 1990b. "Summary of 1990 Census Plans for Enumeration of the Homeless." Washington, D.C.

_____. 1992. *Statistical Abstract of the United States*. Washington, D.C.

Wagner, David. 1993. *Checkerboard Square: Culture and Resistance in a Homeless Community*. Boulder, Colorado: Westview Press.

Wagner, David and Marcia B. Cohen. 1991. "The Power of the People: Homeless Protesters in the Aftermath of Social Movement Participation." *Social Problems* 38(4): 543-561.

Walter, Carol. 1998. Personal communication with Director of Community Services, Community Renewal Team of Hartford, Connecticut.

Waterston, Alisse. 1993. *Street Addicts in the Political Economy*. Philadelphia: Temple University Press.

Watson, Sophie and Helen Austerberry. 1986. *Housing and Homelessness: A Feminist Perspective*. London: Routledge & Kegan Paul.

Weitzman, Beth C., James R. Knickman, and MaryBeth Shinn. 1990. "Pathways to Homelessness among New York City Families." *Journal of Social Issues*. 46 (4) 125-140.

Weller, M. P. I. and P. Jauhar. 1987. "Wandering at Heathrow Airport by the Mentally Unwell." *Medicine, Science and Law* 27: 40-41. Cited in Hopper, Kim, "Symptoms, Survival, and the Redefinition of Public Space: A Feasibility Study of Homeless People at a Metropolitan Airport." *Urban Anthropology* 20(2) (1991): 155-175.

White-Harvey, Robert J. 1993. "Cohousing: A Scandinavian Longhouse, or a Traditional Approach to Modern Housing?" *The Canadian Journal of Native Studies* 13. 1(1993): 69-82.

Whyte, William Foote. 1995. *Street Corner Society: The Social Structure of an Italian Slum.* Chicago: University of Chicago Press.

Williams, Brackette F. 1995. "The Public I/Eye: Conducting Fieldwork to do Homework on Homelessness and Begging in Two U.S. Cities." *Current Anthropology* 36(1): 25-51.

Wiseman, Jacqueline. 1970. *Stations of the Lost.* Chicago: University of Chicago Press.

Wolch, Jennifer and Michael Dear. 1993. *Malign Neglect: Homelessness in an American City.* San Francisco: Jossey-Bass Publishers.

Wolch, Jennifer, Afsaneh Rahimian, and Paul Koegel. 1993. "Daily and Periodic Mobility Patterns of the Urban Homeless." *Professional Geographer* 45(2): 159-169.

Wolch, Jennifer and Stacy Rowe. 1992. "On the Streets: Mobility Paths of the Urban Homeless." *City and Society* 6(2): 115-140.

Wood, D., B. Valdez, T Hayashi, and A. Shen. 1990. "Homeless and Housed Families in Los Angeles: A Study Comparing Demographic, Economic, and Family Function Characteristics." *American Journal of Public Health* 80: 1049-1052.

Wright, James D. and Joel A. Devine. 1992. "Counting the Homeless: The Census Bureau's 'S-Night' in Five U.S. Cities." *Evaluation Review* 16(4): 355-364.

Wright, Talmadge. 1995. "Tranquility City: Self-Organization, Protest, and Collective Gains within a Chicago Homeless Encampment." In *Marginal Spaces,* ed. Michael Peter Smith, 37-68. (Comparative Urban and Community Research, vol. 5.) New Brunswick, New Jersey: Transaction Books.

Zappardino, Pamela H. and Deborah DeBare. 1992. "In Search of Safety: Double Jeopardy for Battered Women." In *Homelessness: New England and Beyond,* ed. Padraig O'Malley. Amherst, Massachusetts: John W. McCormack Institute of Public Affairs.

Index

DATE DUE